SHERWOOD FOREST
and the Dukeries

IAN D. ROTHERHAM

AMBERLEY

About the Author

Professor Ian D. Rotherham is an international authority on cultural and historical aspects of landscapes and is Reader in Tourism & Environmental Change at Sheffield Hallam University. He has appeared in and advised on many documentaries and news programmes including *Panorama* and *Horizon*. His previous books include *Roman Baths in Britain*, also from Amberley. Ian lives in Sheffield.

First published 2013

Amberley Publishing
The Hill, Stroud
Gloucestershire, GL5 4EP

www.amberley-books.com

British Library Cataloguing in Publication Data.
A catalogue record for this book is available from the British Library.

ISBN 978 1 4456 1474 8 (paperback)
ISBN 978 1 4456 1480 9 (ebook)

Typeset in 10pt on 12pt Sabon.
Typesetting and Origination by Amberley Publishing.
Printed in the UK.

Appointed GPSR EU Representative: Easy Access System Europe Oü, 16879218
Address: Mustamäe tee 50, 10621, Tallinn, Estonia
Contact Details: gpsr.requests@easproject.com, +358 40 500 3575

Contents

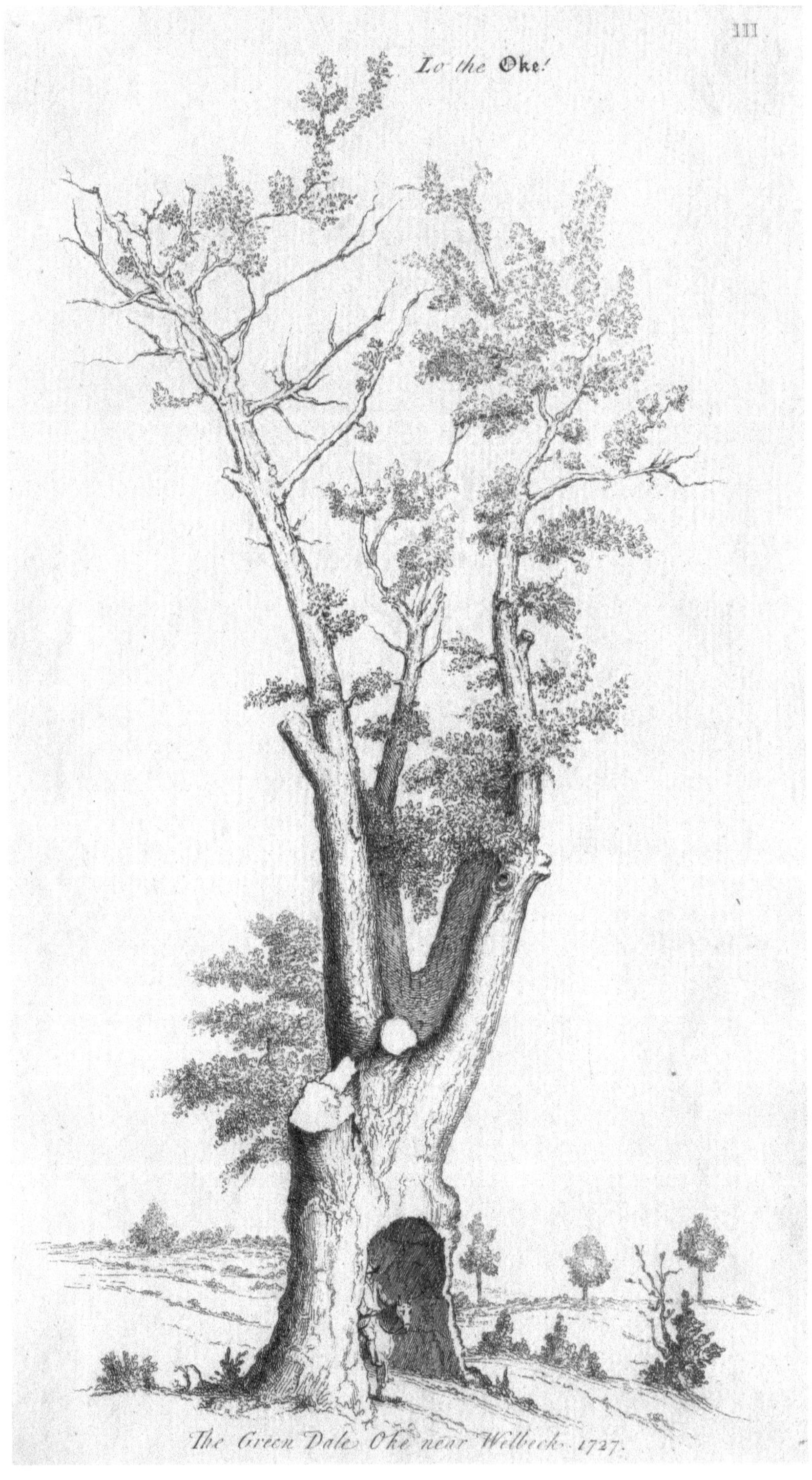

Engraving of the Green Dale Oke near Welbeck, 1727.

PREAMBLE

Sherwood Forest is arguably the most famous historic landscape in the world, immortalised through storytelling, mythology, romantic books, and ultimately by Hollywood. This is the setting for Robin Hood, Little John and the rest of the 'Merry Men'. Yet behind the glamorous legends are equally fascinating places, people and histories. An important and vast medieval 'Forest' and extensive heath, the area was farmed and settled before that time. After the break-up of the Royal Hunting Forest came the famous establishment of great halls, houses and parks of the aristocracy, the so-called 'Dukeries', and then industry, with deep coal mining, wartime military training, and twentieth-century forestry. From the nineteenth century onwards, the region was a notable tourism and leisure destination, and the sites of famous oak trees such as the Major Oak were places one could visit to touch the past. Tourism continues today as visitors from around the world come to experience nature, history and myth.

The region containing Sherwood and the Dukeries, perhaps 40 miles long and 30 miles across, is mostly on red, Bunter or Sherwood Sandstone, which gives rise to heath and acid grassland, and the majestic forest oaks. However, eastwards, the land drops to the Trent Valley with Mercia Mudstones, then alluvial riverine and wetland deposits, with extensive gravels and sands from glacial activity. Large areas are extracted industrially, particularly for gravels, with abandoned sites that are now superb nature reserves, as at Sutton and Lound Gravel Pits, and Attenborough Nature Reserve at Nottingham. West of Sherwood's sandstone core is a ridge of Permian sandstone and mudstone, and Magnesian or Permian limestone running north to south. This gives rise to a landscape of rugged crags like Creswell, limestone grassland and remarkable species-rich woodlands, for example Whitwell and Anston. Further west still, the geology is Coal Measures sandstones and shales, and then Peak District gritstones. The limestone countryside, historically good for farming, forms a high plateau sloping gently eastwards. This belt is different and distinctive from the lands to the west, and separated from the Coal Measures country by the striking escarpment running parallel to the M1 motorway. It is on this spectacular escarpment that both Bolsover Castle and Hardwick Hall stand. The lower-lying Rother Valley is an undulating country of sandstones and shales, with often clay-heavy soils. However, the Coal Measures of the western valleys affect the entire Sherwood region, as they drop deep below ground and the coal-bearing rocks are accessible to deep collieries. The vegetation, the potential of land use in the countryside, and the industrial exploitation of the region are each determined by geology. From prehistory to the present day, the rocks influenced landscape and countryside. For Sherwood, the result is tremendous diversity in a relatively small area. As Roger Redfern points out, Nottinghamshire, and Sherwood in particular, is dominated by the colour brown in its various hues, from dark, peaty or clay soils in the lowlands, to the sandy heaths of Sherwood on higher ground. The heather, bracken and oaks, in their wood and then in their autumn shades, give us the browns and golds of this soft, rich landscape. If we look from the high ground of the South Pennines and Peak District, then all this area is lowland, with the pale yellow of the Magnesian limestone ridge dominating the foreground and separating the lower lands of Sherwood and beyond.

The watercourses generally follow this pattern, and are mostly small, sluggish streams, meandering across flat catchments. Some, such as at Welbeck Great Lake, or Clumber Park, have been harnessed to create water bodies out of proportion to the modest streams that feed them. The exception is the River Trent, which drains a huge part of middle England and sweeps majestically to the south and then east of our region. Look eastwards, and the power stations such as Ratcliffe mark out the path of the county's major river. The smaller watercourses wend their ways eastwards to meet and merge with Trent, and eventually discharge into the great Humber Estuary.

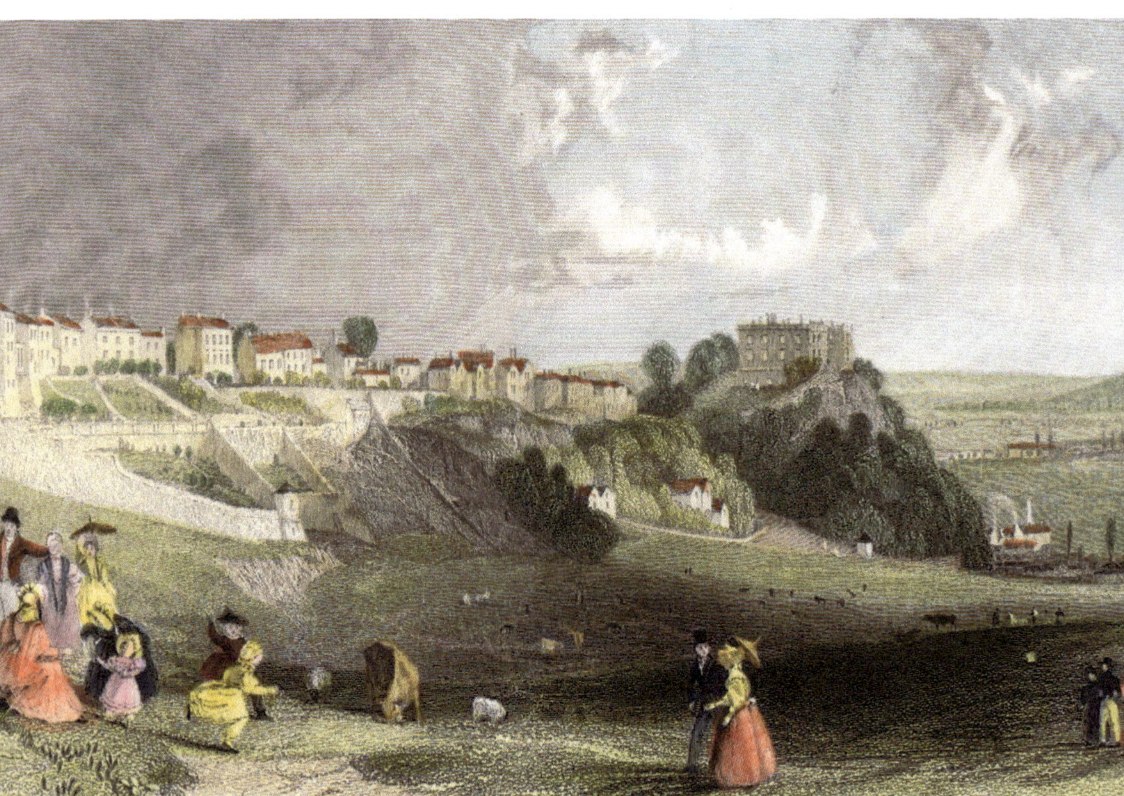

Nottingham Park and the castle in the 1700s.

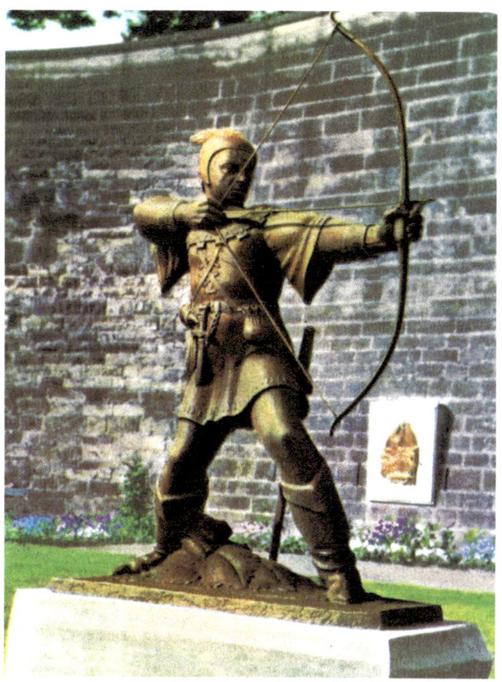

Statue of Robin Hood at Nottingham Castle, now a major tourist feature.

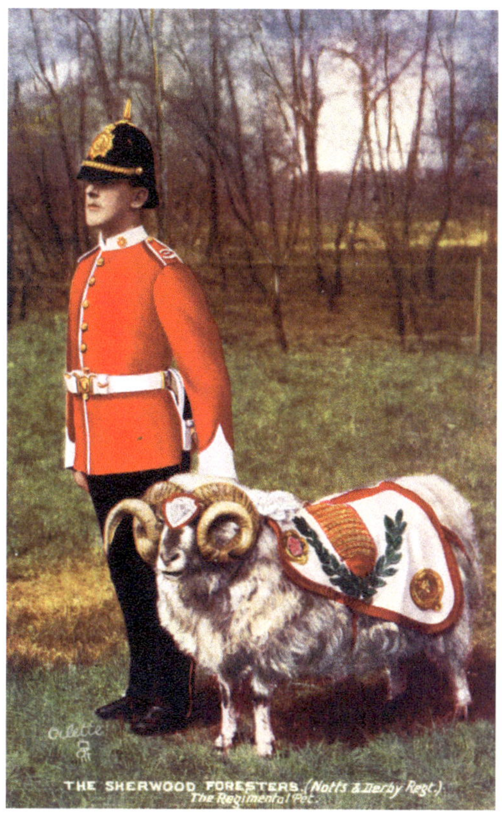

The Sherwood Foresters and ceremonial ram, early 1900s.

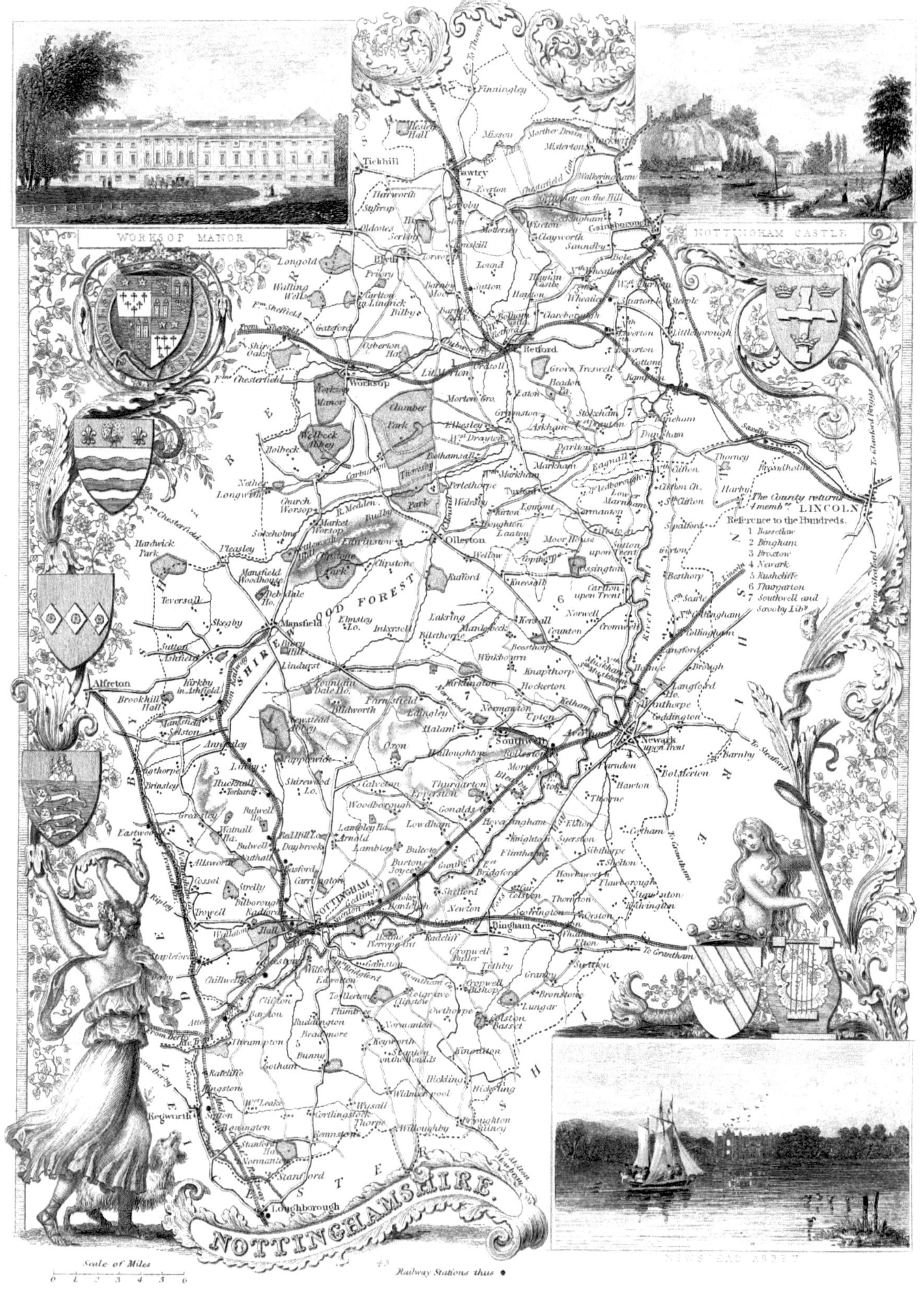

Map of Nottinghamshire and the Dukeries in the early 1800s.

I

ANCIENT, HISTORIC AND REMARKABLE LANDSCAPE: SHERWOOD FOREST AND THE DUKERIES

Central to the story is the Royal Forest of Sherwood. However, contrary to popular myth, a Royal Forest was an area of land that might in fact have relatively few trees, vastly different from the idea of the 'forestry' that today covers much of the area. The ancient forest was mostly open oak and birch heath apart from two main areas: between Nottingham and Mansfield, and north from Edwinstowe to Ollerton. In these was denser woodland, with both sessile and English oaks. The origin of the name 'Sherwood' is not clear, though wood is from *wudu*, the Old English for extensively wooded landscape. 'Sher' may be from 'shire', i.e. the county's wood, or 'bright' or 'famous'. Sherwood as the 'Shire-Wood' seems reasonable. The forest boundaries seem to have varied considerably over time, and in 1218, Henry III despatched a jury of knights and freemen to ride the perimeter of the Royal Forest. They went as far as Southwell and Laxton in the south-east, and to the outskirts of Chesterfield in the north-west. Ideas of the intractable forest reaching all the way to western locations, such as the Peak District and Chatsworth, are modern, fanciful illusions. The forest was divided into 'Thorney-wood', or scrubby, oak–birch woodland, and 'High Forest', or mature oaks and little understorey.

Forestry is a relatively modern concept, developed in Germany and France during the eighteenth and nineteenth centuries, and is the management of timber trees as 'high forest', often with exotic species imported and planted. The 'Forest' on the other hand was a legal system of land management evolved in Continental Europe and imported to England by Norman invaders. It was designed to promote and protect the hunting interests and resources of great tracts of land. This is not to say that the Anglo-Saxons were not great hunters, they were. However, in Anglo-Saxon England, while the kings were great huntsmen, they did not set aside areas *outside* (Latin – *foris*) the law of the land and subject to special controls. They created some large deer parks, but in the wider landscape, game ran freely and areas were not especially protected. Under the Norman kings, by royal prerogative, Forest Law was widely applied to areas that were forests, i.e. outside the law of the land. It was the punitive aspects of these laws that became the stuff of folklore and legend, up to modern-day Hollywood. According to the law, a local man caught stealing a wild boar, for example, might have his eyes put out, a strong disincentive!

The particular laws applied within the forests intended to protect and conserve venison and vert. The laws applied particularly to the animals of the chase or hunt: red, roe, and fallow deer and wild boar, and the vegetation or vert (greenery) upon which they fed. The Normans, specifically for the chase, reintroduced fallow deer, a Mediterranean species originally brought to Britain by the Romans. The designated forests were hunting areas reserved for the monarch and, by invitation or gift only, the aristocracy. This idea of land management was introduced to England by the Normans and gave rise to many of the real complaints from Saxon commoners about repressive overlordship. This is also the stuff of Hollywood myth, and in reality, in many cases Forest Laws were applied in order to exact fines and raise revenue for the Crown, which was usually short of money. Understanding the forest, its history and its impacts on landscape and on local people is central to our wider story of Sherwood Forest and the Dukeries. Even today, otherwise reliable authors on the area seem to think this was a landscape of impenetrable trees, of wall-to-wall, dark and secretive 'forest'. In Kevin Costner's *Robin Hood: Prince of Thieves*, the outlaws' Sherwood home is constructed in a mature stand of beech, a tree that did not arrive in the area until it was planted perhaps in the 1700s. Other sites include typical conifer plantations of the 1800s and 1900s. Yet Sherwood Forest was an extensive and expansive heathland, with wide open vistas and large numbers of giant oaks, open-grown trees spaced widely apart.

Offences Within the Forest

There were two categories of offences under Forest Law. 1) Trespass against the vert (forest vegetation) and 2) Trespass against the venison (the game). With regard to the latter, there were five forest animals protected by law: the hart and hind (red deer), boar, hare and wolf. Of these, in England, the boar was extinct by the thirteenth century, though is excitingly now in the process of re-establishment. The wolf had gone from England by the late fifteenth century. There was further protection extended to 1) The beasts of chase: the buck and doe (fallow deer), fox, marten, and roe deer, and 2) The beasts and fowls of warren: the hare, coney, pheasant, and partridge. However, rights of chase and of free warren (i.e. to hunt such animals) were often granted to local nobility for a fee or for services rendered, often in a park or a chase, and set alongside, but separate from, the forests.

There were numerous 'trespasses' against the vert. These transgressions included *purpresture*, or the enclosure of pasture or erection of buildings on forestlands, *assarting*, or clearing forestland for agriculture, and felling trees or clearing shrubs. Importantly, the laws and the associated offences applied to all lands inside the forest boundary, even those privately owned. In 1217, *The Charter of the Forest* established that all freemen owning land within the forest enjoyed the rights of *agistment* and *pannage*.

Dwellers in the forest were prohibited from bearing hunting weapons, and potential hunting dogs were banned from forest. However, in an age where security and locks were basic and primitive, mastiffs were allowed as guard dogs, but only if they had their front claws removed to render them useless for hunting. Lands on the edge of the designated forest were called *purlieus* and agriculture was permitted. Deer escaping from the forest into these areas could be killed if they caused damage. Potentially, if these laws were broken, offenders would have their hands struck off, or be blinded in both eyes. In practice, the solution was generally a fine. Sometimes, however, there was serious violence between those breaching the regulations and those charged with enforcement.

Rights and Privileges in the Forest

The sovereign and the Crown estate realised that money could be raised by fines and through allocation of rights for fees to provide much-needed income. For example, nobles could be granted royal licence to take game. Local commoners held various rights associated with their village or dwelling. These included *estover*, the right of taking firewood, *pannage*, the hugely important right to pasture swine in the forest, *turbary*, the right to cut turf or peat (as fuel), and various assorted rights of pasturage (*agistment*). They could harvest various forest products and take small wood as needed for building and perhaps fuel. Timber, from big trees, was reserved for the Crown. The land could be disafforested in part or entirely, and permission given for *assart* and *purpresture* (encroachment).

The Forest Courts

The administration of these difficult laws required a legal system to adjudicate and to enforce action: the Forest Courts. The senior Forest Court was the Court of Justice-seat or Eyre, held every three years, and announced forty days before sitting. Presided over by a Justice in Eyre, it was, in theory at least, the only court that passed sentence on offenders. However, in practice, these distinctions were often overlooked with a degree of pragmatism varying from forest to forest. Since Courts of Justice-seat were only infrequent, lower courts assumed the power to fine offenders according to fixed charges. The Courts of Justice-seat declined, and the Office of Justice was abolished in 1817, its powers passing to the First Commissioner of Woods and Forests. Understanding the basics of this system and its administration is at the heart of an awareness of how medieval Sherwood might have looked and functioned. This is the real landscape of Robin Hood, rather than the Hollywood myth.

The status of the forests varied with the fortunes and stability of the Crown, the barons, and the vagaries of hunting fashions. By the Tudors, it was clear that Forest Law was largely anachronistic and its prime purpose was now to protect timber in the Royal Forests. However, this role should not be dismissed lightly since access to big timber trees was vital for building, and for national security in constructing warships. The forests remained economically significant to the Crown. James I, for example, enquired into *assart* lands (i.e. private individuals enclosing and cultivating open land in the forest) and the enquiry, with appointed commissioners, generated over £25,000 from occupiers; ownership was confirmed but subject to a fixed annual rent. Similarly, in disputes with Parliament, Charles I was perpetually under financial strain, and several forests were dissaforested. The king gained part of the 'waste land' of the forest, which he could then sell. Following this pattern, nationally, the last major application of Forest Law, by a Court of Justice-seat or forest Eyre, around 1635, was to raise money.

In the late 1780s, a royal commission enquired into the condition of Crown woods. By this time, north of the River Trent, only Sherwood Forest still survived. Since few of the remaining forests had swainmote courts, there was no official supervision or control of activities. The remaining forests were divided into those owned by the Crown and those owned by aristocrats. Where most of the soil belonged to the Crown, lands were reserved to produce oak for shipbuilding, and others were to be enclosed. In these latter cases, the Crown received an allotment of the lands in compensation for loss of rights. Then, in 1810, responsibility for woods passed from the surveyors general (responsible to the auditors of land revenue), to a new Commissioner of Woods, Forests, and Land Revenues, and between 1832 and 1851, 'Works and Buildings' became part of their wider remit. However, in 1851, the commissioner reverted to being a Commissioner of Woods, Forests and Land Revenues. Finally, following establishment of the Forestry Commission in 1919, in 1924, Royal Forests transferred to the new authority. The blanket afforestation of much of the forest area of sites like Sherwood reflects this latter phase. Throughout the twentieth century, many such lands were also set aside for the use of the Army for military training. Indeed, in parts of Sherwood, until quite recent times, signs warned drivers to be alert for Chieftain tanks crossing the road!

Sherwood Forest and the Dukeries

This region has been a major visitor destination for over two centuries. Drawn by landscape and hunting, by great houses, halls, and estates, and ultimately by Victorian romantic legends, tourists flocked to the area and especially its ancient trees. Victorian politician Benjamin Disraeli had close connections here and wrote a description based on a typical Sherwood scene, and many parts of Sherwood still evoke a similar reaction:

> … a fragment of one of those vast sylvan tracts wherein Norman kings once hunted and Saxon outlaws plundered; and although the plough had for centuries successfully invaded brake and bower, the relics retain all their original character of wildness and seclusion. Sometimes the green earth was thickly studded with groves of huge and vigorous oaks, intersected with those smooth and sunny glades that seem as if they must be cut for dames and knights to saunter on. The landscape, still strictly sylvan, would beautifully expand with every combination and variety of woodland; while in the centre, the wildfowl covered the waters of a lake, and the deer basked on the knolls that abounded on its banks.

Sherwood relates to the once vast Royal Forest of medieval England, and the Dukeries' name derives from the great ducal estates that followed the break-up of the forest. We owe the survival of the landscape Disraeli described to these great estates, and, today, bodies like the National Trust. The region covered by the term was that of five great estates – Worksop Manor, Welbeck Abbey, Clumber Park, Thoresby, and to the north, Kiveton, the estate of the dukes of Leeds. Close to Clumber was an earlier home of the Holles, who became the dukes of Newcastle at Clumber. This sixth estate had a grand house, a deer park and pleasure grounds close to the River Idle. Sadly, today nothing remains at all. There is also Rufford Abbey, which is still a major site but, like Clumber, has lost its great buildings. These were aristocratic estates hewn from the expansive wooded heath of Sherwood. Today areas of heath and great trees survive, though much reduced.

Sherwood Forest and the Dukeries have Nottingham to the south, Mansfield to the west, Retford to the east, and Worksop to the north. With its richly romantic attachments, Edwinstowe lies at the heart of the region. Close by, Creswell Crags, now a World Heritage Site, has some of the oldest evidence of human occupation in Britain. This reinforces the feeling of timelessness in the Sherwood landscape – it takes one beyond the medieval and back to the prehistoric. In the west is the heavily industrial area of Mansfield, until the 1990s one of Britain's main centres for deep-mined coal. To the east and the north lies rich, fertile farming and in the valley of the River Trent, and until recent centuries, a vast wetland. This landscape of stark contrasts has surprising endurance and continuity. Sherwood itself sits mostly on poor land, on free-draining, acidic sandstone. This environment resisted attempts at more intensive farming, so its primary value for many centuries was as a boundless and extensive 'forest' – a Royal Hunting Preserve. The Sherwood of both history and legend thus emerged. Walk through this landscape and you tread in the very footsteps of Robin Hood.

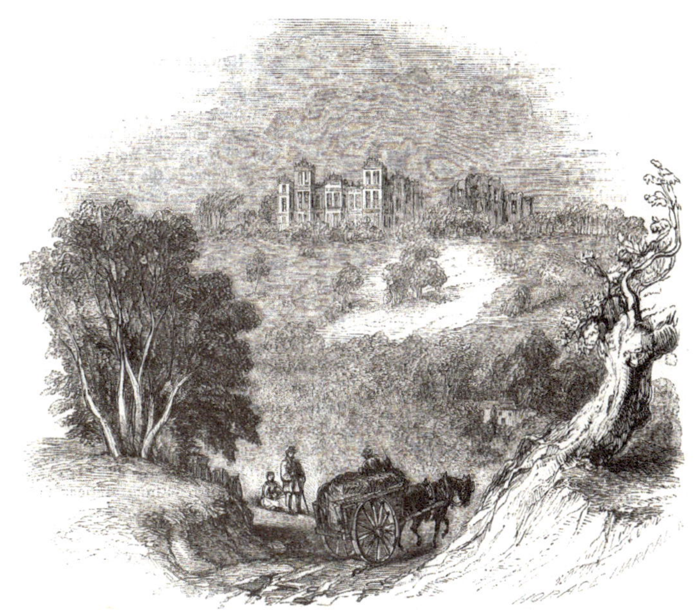

Old and New Hardwick Halls viewed from the valley below and now crossed by the M1 motorway.

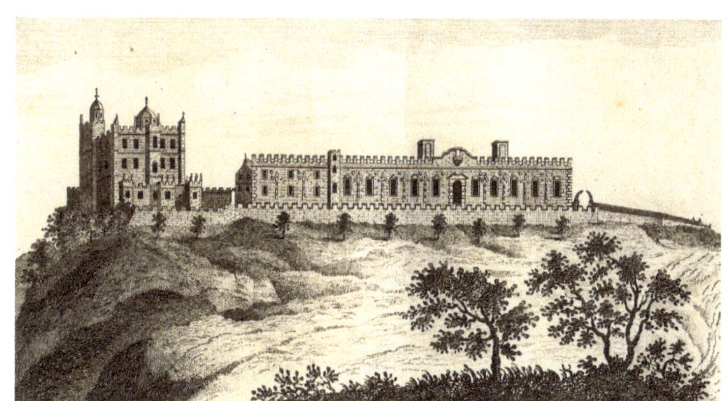

View of Bolsover Castle in Derbyshire as seen from the M1.

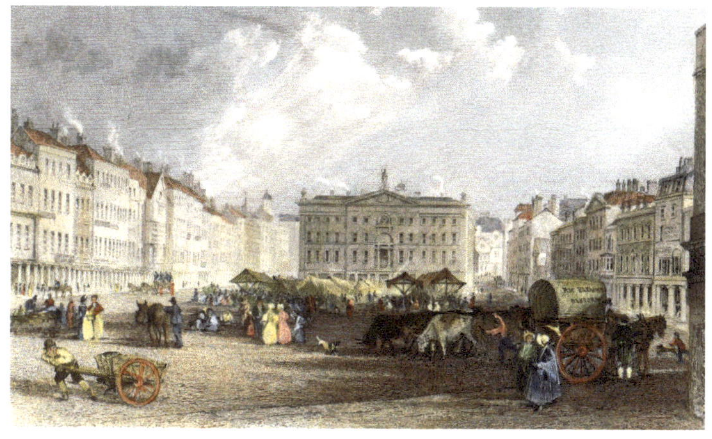

Market Place, Nottingham, in the early 1800s.

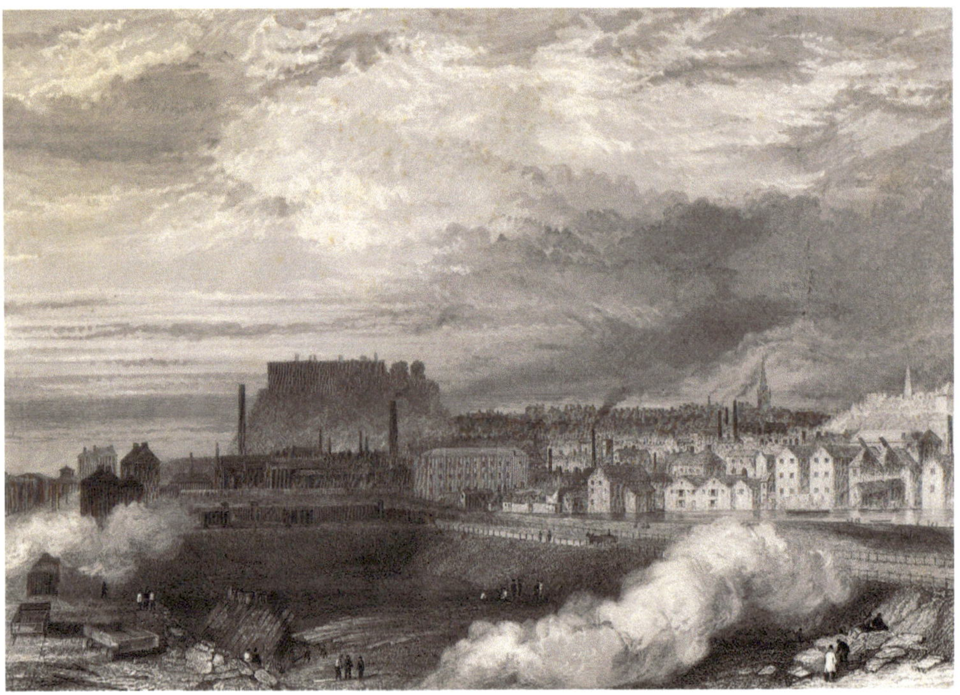

View of Nottingham, the industrialising city, 1800s.

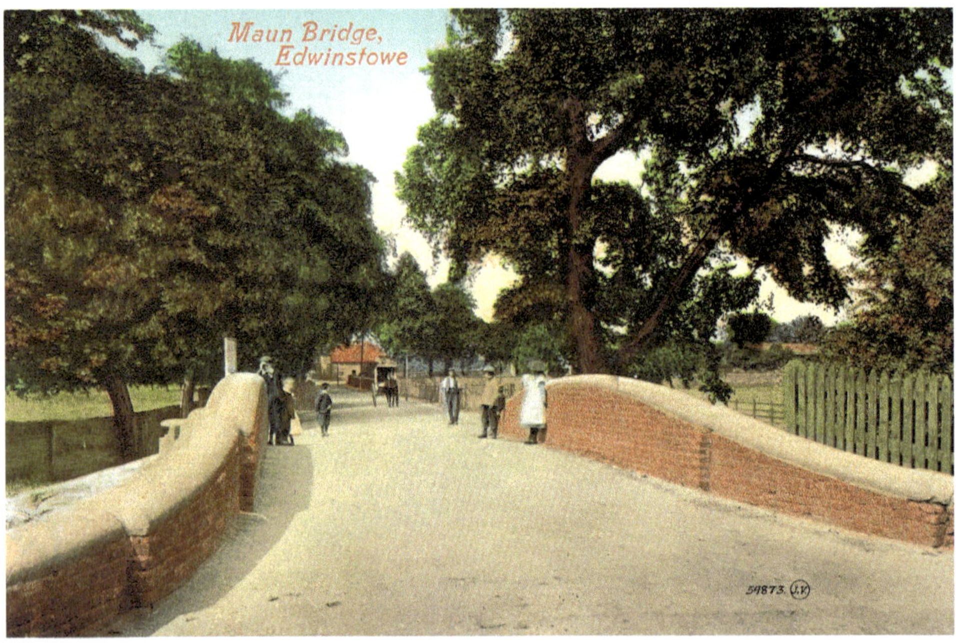

Maun Bridge, Edwinstowe, 1910.

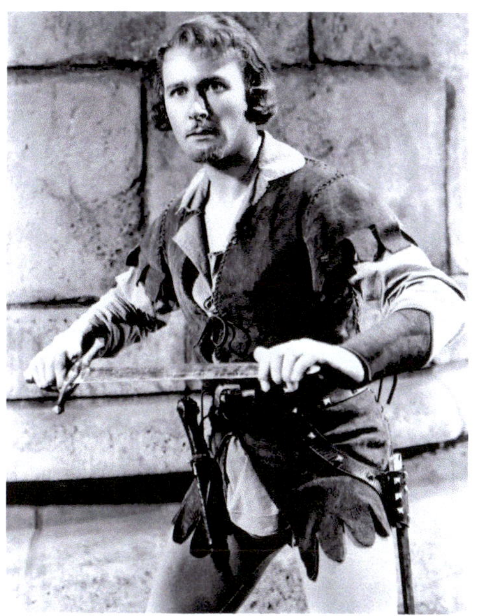 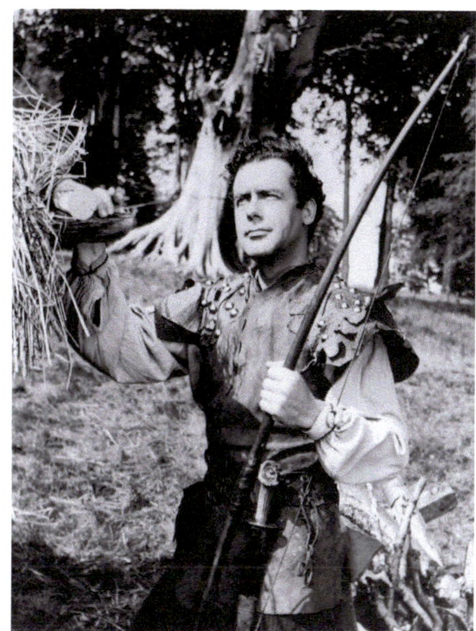

Above left: Errol Flynn as Robin Hood in the 1938 film.

Above right: Richard Green as 1960s television favourite Robin Hood; in the opening sequence the arrow flies past a telegraph pole!

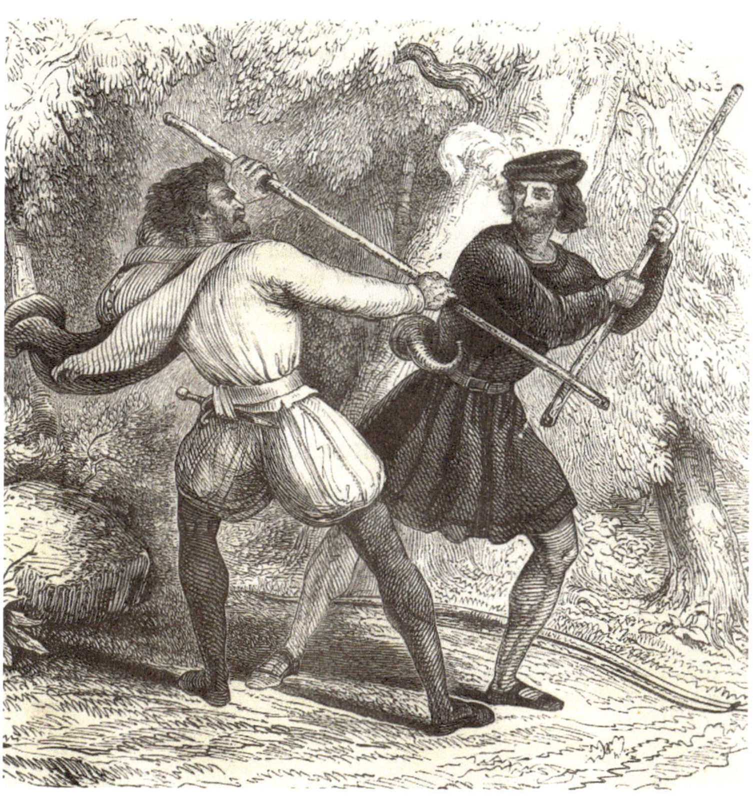

Robin Hood and the Tanner fighting with quarterstaffs.

2

Some Key Places of Sherwood and the Dukeries

Clipstone

Around 2 miles south-west of Edwinstowe and 5 miles north-east of Mansfield, the small village of Clipstone belies its regal past and traditions. As quoted in Sisson's *Beauties of Sherwood Forest*,

> No more the sound of bugle horn
> Shall rouse the outlaw band;
>
> And quarry, and hawk, and deer-hound good,
> And minstrel's gentle lay –
> All these from old Sherwoods' forest glades
> Long time have passed away!

Old Clipstone or King's Clipstone, dating back to Domesday, was for over two centuries the meeting place and sporting centre for the Plantagenet kings of England. Like so many villages across Sherwood and the Dukeries, Clipstone changed dramatically with twentieth-century coal mining and military training.

Creswell Crags

Often described as a miniature Cheddar Gorge, Creswell Crags is a remarkable and even unique site. It is a limestone gorge, honeycombed with caves that were occupied by early humans, and in which archaeologists have found stone tools and animal remains. These remarkable finds evidence the times of the last Ice Age, around 50,000 to 10,000 years ago. The caves contain diverse materials from a wide range of periods, from Stone Age (Upper Palaeolithic and Mesolithic), to Neolithic, Bronze Age, Roman and post-medieval. The rocks gave rise to the caves themselves, but also to the process whereby the archaeological remains were preserved. Limestone is alkaline and dissolves in slightly acid rainwater. Not only did this form the caves, but also, as mineral-rich water continued to drip down into the caves and onto sediments in the cave floors, the mineral was re-deposited. This meant that over millennia, delicate bones and artefacts were sealed and protected under layers of concrete. If you are fortunate enough to witness today's archaeologists at work, you will see them excavate these precious sediments one cubic centimetre at a time. When the pioneering Victorian diggers went in, they hired men with dynamite to blow up the concreted sediments, and then they extracted materials with pick and shovel.

People lived here from around 43,000 BC, and again about 30,000 to 28,000 BC and, more recently, nearly 12,000 years ago. The archaeological finds have included a bone engraved with a horse's head, various worked bone items, plus numerous bones of prehistoric animals. Many of these were found in excavations from 1876 up to the present day. A carved bone discovered in 1876 is Britain's only piece of Upper Palaeolithic portable art showing an animal. The Robin Hood Cave Horse was previously known as the Ochre Horse, and is a fragment of rib engraved with a horse's head dating from between 11,000 and 13,000 years ago. In the 1920s, a further important find was that of the Pinhole Cave Man, a human figure engraved on bone.

In April 2003, the discovery of engravings and bas-reliefs on the walls and ceilings of some of the caves was truly momentous. Until this time, it was believed there was no cave art in Britain. The images at Creswell include animals such as bison and perhaps birds, though these may be human female representations. The engravings are based on the naturally uneven surfaces of the cave walls and stand out best in particular lights, such as in the early morning.

There are numerous occupied caves at Creswell, and perhaps others which have yet to be discovered. Mother Grundy's Parlour, with many flint tools and split bones, was occupied until the Mesolithic. Evidence from Robin Hood's Cave, suggests the occupants hunted and trapped woolly rhinoceroses and arctic hares. The Pin Hole Cave had a prehistoric hyena den and was home to Neanderthals. Church Hole, occupied intermittently until Roman times, has over eighty wall engravings.

Creswell Crags is a Site of Special Scientific Interest (SSSI), and in 2006, the B6042 road was diverted from its route through the Crags gorge to minimise traffic impact on the site. Visitors can once again enjoy its sites and prehistoric character unfettered by cars. There is an excellent visitor centre, and the car park makes a good base to explore the Robin Hood Way.

Eakring

This is a small village between Ollerton to the north and Southwell to the south, and famous for having as its vicar the Reverend William Mompesson, formerly vicar of Eyam during the Plague in 1666. He moved to the village of Eakring as rector in 1670, and lived there for thirty-nine years, and his body is buried in the churchyard. The Eakring parish church, built in the thirteenth, fourteenth and fifteenth centuries, was restored in the early 1880s, and is dedicated to St Andrew. On his arrival at Eakring, Mompesson was viewed with suspicion by the locals, and after his induction, they would not allow him to preach within the church itself. Instead, for some time he was compelled to live in a hut in Rufford Park and to preach his sermons in the open air, at a location still called 'Pulpit Ash'. Yet despite this 'welcome', he stayed in the parish for many years and died there in 1708.

Edwinstowe

This small town, of about 5,000 people, lies at the centre of the forest and was where Robin and Maid Marion reputedly married. In the Domesday Book of 1086, it was described thus: 'In Edenstow is a Berewick of one Caricute of land to be taxed, land to two ploughs, there is a Church and a priest, and four bordars have one plough, wood pasture half a mile long and half broad.' However, the story of Edwinstowe goes further back and has a a tragic royal connection. This was the site of the temporary burial of St Edwin, King of Northumbria, following the Battle of Heathfield in the Humberhead Levels in 633. To mark the historic site in Edwinstowe, there was probably a church built of Sherwood oak on a base of sandstone over the resting place. In 1951, the National Coal Board extended mining operations to just beneath St Mary's church, Cuckney. In order to reinforce the church foundations, building work was necessary and this began with the digging six trenches across the nave. Excavations revealed large amounts of bone, perhaps from the soldiers who died with their king. It was a remarkable discovery of over 200 skeletons, all young men, buried together and conveying the idea of soldiers from a battle. Because of the haste of the contracted works, there was no time for archaeological investigation of the sort that would be demanded today for such an important find.

The battle was hugely significant in English history since it pitched the powerful Northumbrian king, recently converted to Christianity, against an alliance of pagans. Edwin at the time was the most powerful ruler in Britain, and appeared to have defeated Cadwallon a few years previously. The Northumbrian force was led by Edwin, and that of the alliance of Gwynedd (North Wales) and Mercia, by Cadwallon ap Cadfan and Penda, who became the last pagan English king. The battlefield was a marshy area north-east of Doncaster on the south bank of the River Don. The battle was a decisive victory for Gwynedd and Mercia, and caused the short-term collapse of Northumbria, the kingdom temporarily split into sub-kingdoms. With his army defeated, both Edwin and his son Osfrith were killed, and his other son, Eadfrith, was captured and later killed by Penda. Cadwallon continued to slaughter Northumbrians until a year later, when Oswald finally defeated him. The Christian Oswald thus became King of Northumbria and reunited the kingdoms of Bernicia and Deira once again under a single ruler.

Edwinstowe was always at the core of forest activities, and, within the forest, was subject to Forest Law, causing conflicts and unrest. Interestingly, these often involved the clergy, as in 1334, for example, when Vicar John de Ryston was convicted of venison trespass. Then in 1340, Vicar Thomas Fox, son of Henry de Edenstowe, was imprisoned at Nottingham for 'trespass of vert in Sherwood Forest'.

In 1907, Revd Edward V. Bond became the new vicar at Edwinstowe and brought with him an interest in local history and archaeology. He found the site of St Edwin's Chapel and hermitage in the forest near to King's Clipstone. Founded by King John, this was a chantry dedicated to the souls of his family, and for all whom he had wronged – probably quite a few people! In 1918, Reverend Frank Cecil Day-Lewis became vicar, and his son, Cecil Day-Lewis, was a young man at university, later to become poet laureate. He wrote in his memoirs:

> When my father moved to Edwinstowe, it was a country village ... before he died, it had become a mining town ... We lived on coal. Seams of it lay below our feet – rich seams which had hardly been tapped yet ... and my father's stipend of £600 a year came largely, I believe, from the titled patron of the living, beneath whose land the coal had been found.

In a thousand years, Edwinstowe changed from rural forest location and host to a royal court, to a centre for coal mining.

Laxton & the Open Fields

Laxton village is uniquely important in English landscape and farming history. Its claim to fame is as one of the last working open field systems in the country. There are others at Braunton in Devon and near the Isle of Axholme in the Humberhead Levels. The relict land management system of Laxton is almost unique, a last vestige of England's medieval landscape. Today the area and its administration are protected by a Parliamentary undertaking from the Crown Estate Commissioners when they purchased Laxton Estate in 1981. There is an Environmental Stewardship agreement with Natural England and the manor court leet to protect the 'sykes', four areas of open fields also designated Sites of Special Scientific Interest (SSSI). The rest of the estate is ordinary, conventional farmland, but the fields, divided into strips, are used in common by the villagers. Three open fields, the Mill Field, the South Field and the West Field, remain. In 1635, Mark Pierce undertook a survey of the parish and the document is now in the Bodleian Library. This shows the three fields, in use at that time, but larger than today. A fourth field was farmed as a part of the West Field, and the East Field was smaller than the others were and remains today enclosed and managed as a number of small, individual fields.

Mansfield

Along with early English kings who stayed in Mansfield to hunt in Sherwood, it is believed that the Mercian kings came here for hunting. Around 12 miles north of Nottingham, Mansfield is in low-lying ground surrounded by steep hills in the Maun Valley. Today it is largely urban, with around 100,000 residents. Most people live in Mansfield or Mansfield Woodhouse, but Market Warsop and Church Warsop are also popular residential areas. These towns were once pretty, rural centres amid attractive, productive, rolling countryside, but during the last century have suffered dramatic impacts of industrialisation and urbanisation.

Whitwell

South-west of Worksop, Whitwell is a small town on the magnesian limestone ridge, lying just north of Creswell Crags. Like so many small Dukeries settlements, it has many charming old houses but suffered from mass housing for imported mine workers. Today it is discovering a new era of post-industrial life. Whitwell Wood is claimed to be the biggest 'wood' in Europe, and there are Iron Age burial mounds, an Iron Age fort and settlement, remains of a Romano-British villa, medieval field systems and green lanes, and both Norman and Saxon churches. The splendid Whitwell Old Hall is a medieval manor house. St Lawrence church dates from 1200 and boasts one of the most impressive Norman naves in Derbyshire, surely a marker of earlier prosperity.

Worksop

Now with around 60,000 people, located to the north of our region, Worksop is regarded as the 'Gateway to the Dukeries'. At Domesday, it was Wirchesop, maybe after the ancient fortification, or 'work', just north of the town centre on Castle Hill. Alternatively, it may be named after a local Saxon noble called Weore. A small market town close to the Dukeries estates, Worksop was the location of the priory and then Worksop Manor. While it still has some remarkable historic buildings and other features, it suffered badly during the Industrial Revolution and is now re-emerging after the closure of the coal mines. Of Norman construction, the priory church of Our Lady and St Cuthbert is probably the town's most splendid ancient building, and has a large gatehouse. The Norman priory was part of an Augustinian monastery founded in 1103, replacing an earlier parish church. The nave of the original monastic structure, completed in 1170, was around 360 feet long, compared to the present-day structure of around 135 feet. Sir William de Lovetot, the Lord of the Manor of Worksop, founded the priory and dedicated it to St Cuthbert. Our Lady, the Virgin Mary, was a later addition. The de Lovetots and their descendants, the de Furnivals and Nevills, were active in the Crusades and supported the priory. At Dissolution the buildings were ransacked and all that remains of the effigies are three mutilated statues of Lord Furnival, his sister and his brother-in-law. There were close links between the lordships of Worksop and of Sheffield and the two towns remained closely associated throughout history. Despite the Dissolution, the priory church is largely intact, probably because it also functioned as the parish church. Remarkably, when many Catholic shrines were pillaged and destroyed, the gatehouse and shrine survived. The gatehouse is late thirteenth century and is a particularly interesting building. Even the external statues of St Augustine, St Cuthbert and other religious images are intact in their wall niches.

Along with some significant Victorian buildings is the half-timbered Old Ship Inn, the oldest pub in Worksop. This reputedly has wooden beams from ships that fought in the Battle of Trafalgar. There are also rumours of connecting passages to the Welbeck estate and a priest hole, or hidden recess, where Catholic priests could hide. Worksop Market dates back to 1296, with a charter from Edward for a market on the Feast of St Cuthbert. The market remains a distinctive feature of the town, every week on Wednesday, Friday and Saturday, with a rich array of stalls and stallholders.

Just south of Worksop is Worksop College, a long-standing private school with a magnificent building and extensive grounds.

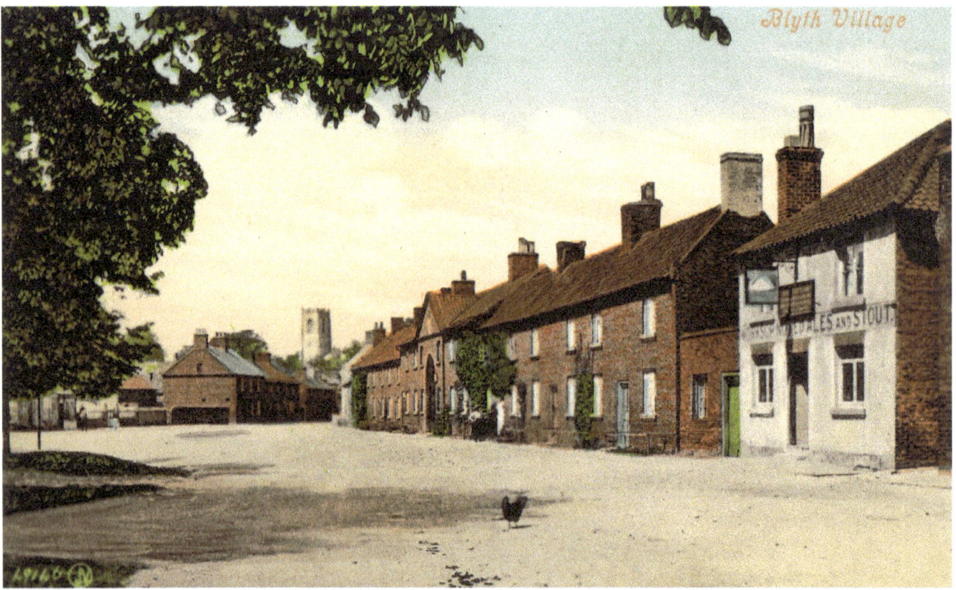

Blyth village near Hodsock Priory, 1906.

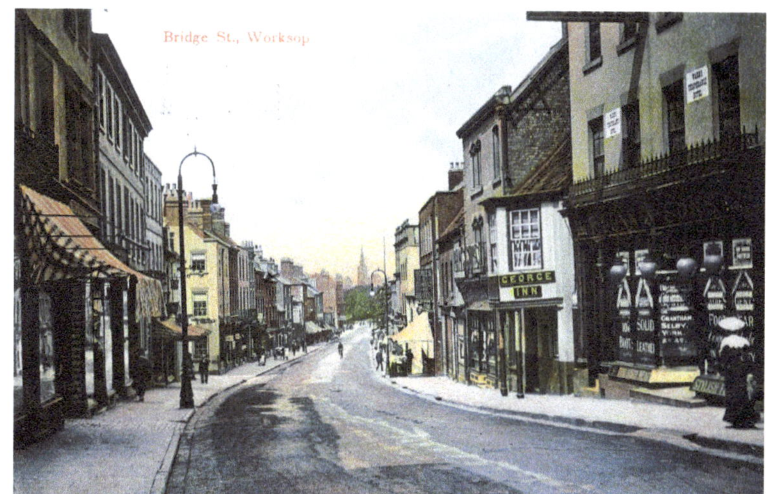

Bridge Street in the busy town of Worksop, 1908.

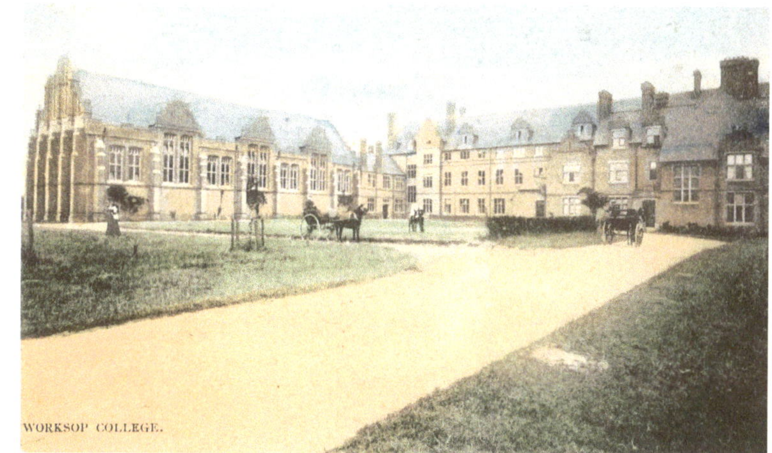

Worksop College, an exclusive school in the shadow of industrial coal mining and great ducal estates.

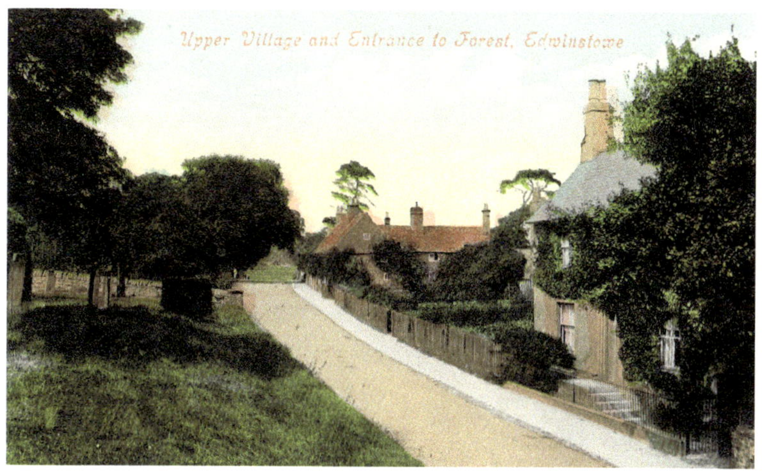

Edwinstowe upper village and entrance to Sherwood Forest.

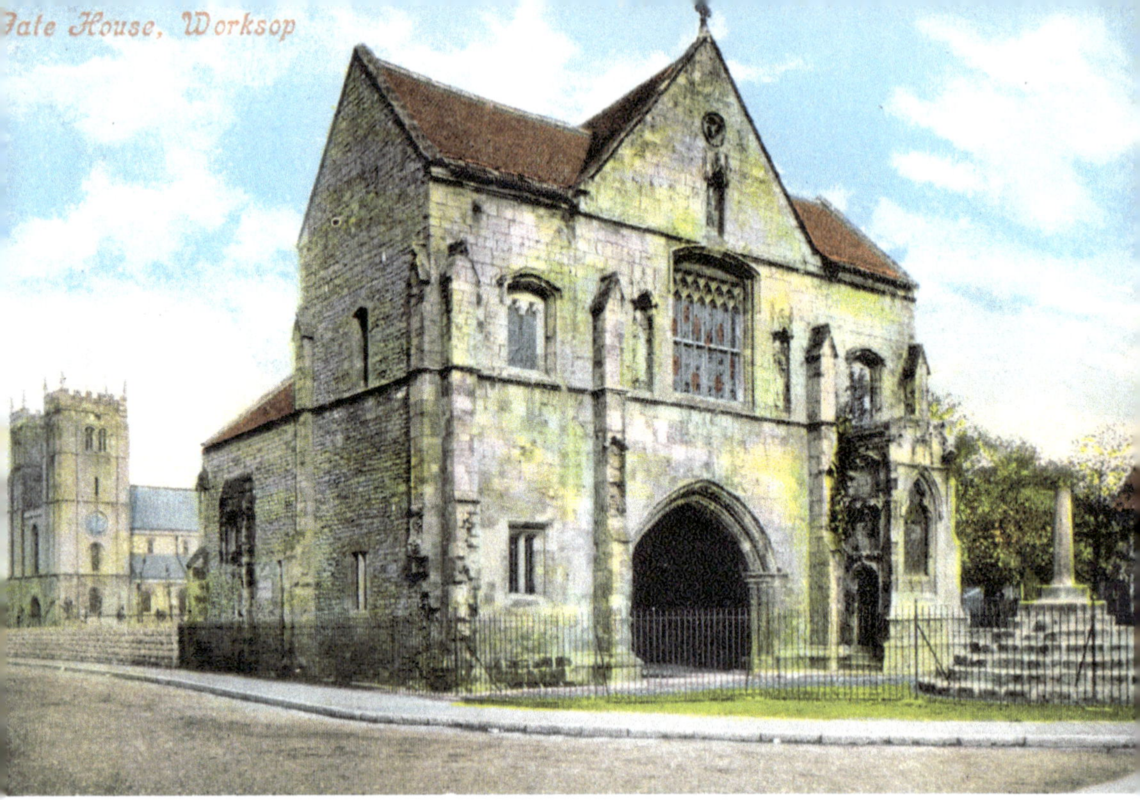

Gatehouse, Worksop, early 1900s.

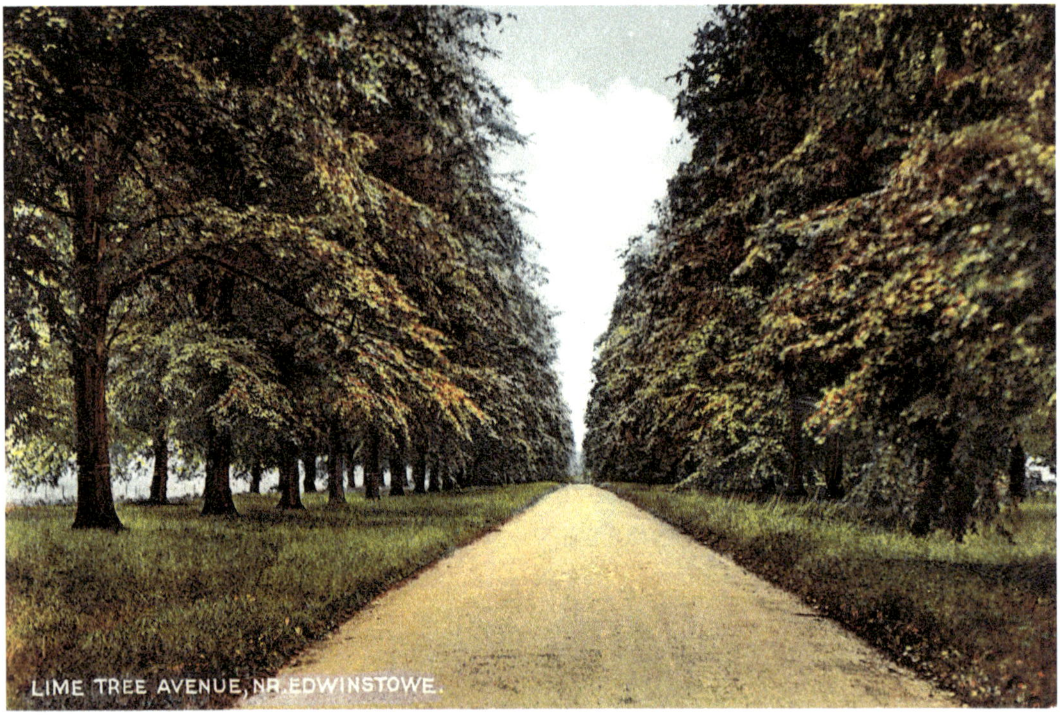

Lime Tree Avenue, Clumber, near Edwinstowe.

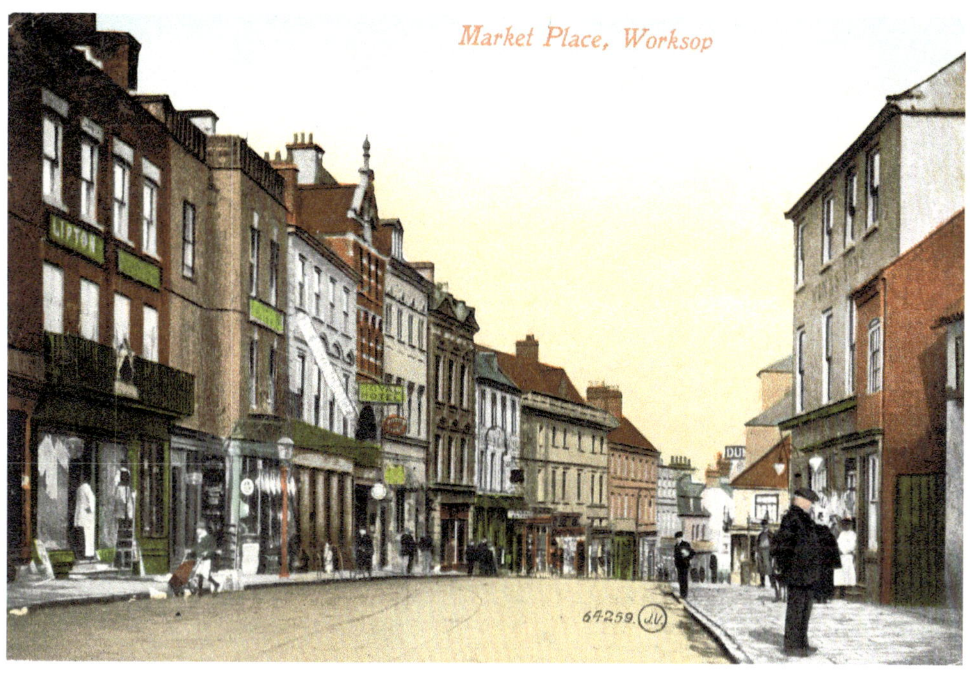

Market Place in Worksop, which still boasts a regular and popular market.

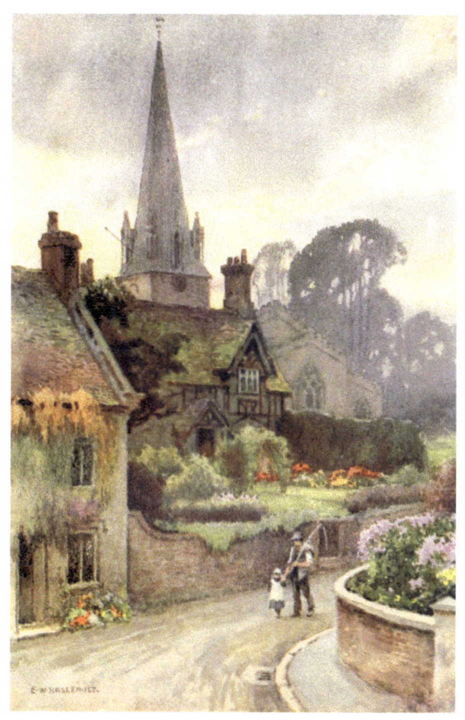

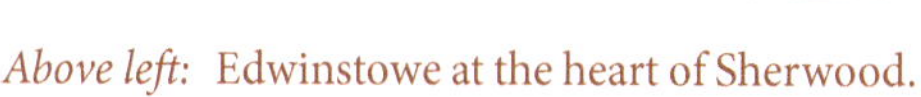

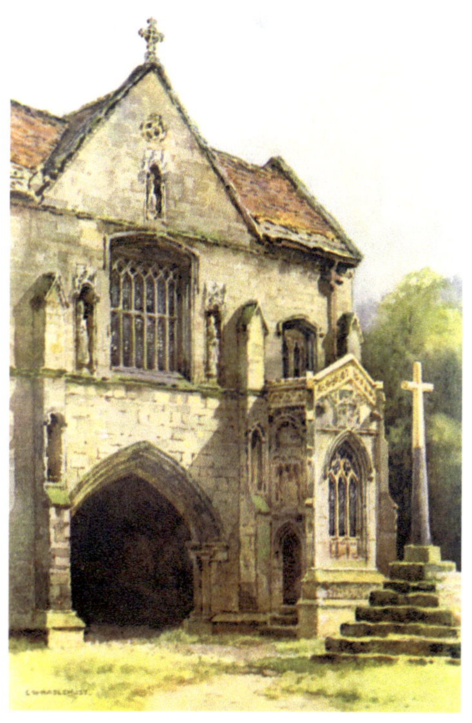

Above left: Edwinstowe at the heart of Sherwood.

Above right: Priory Gateway, Worksop.

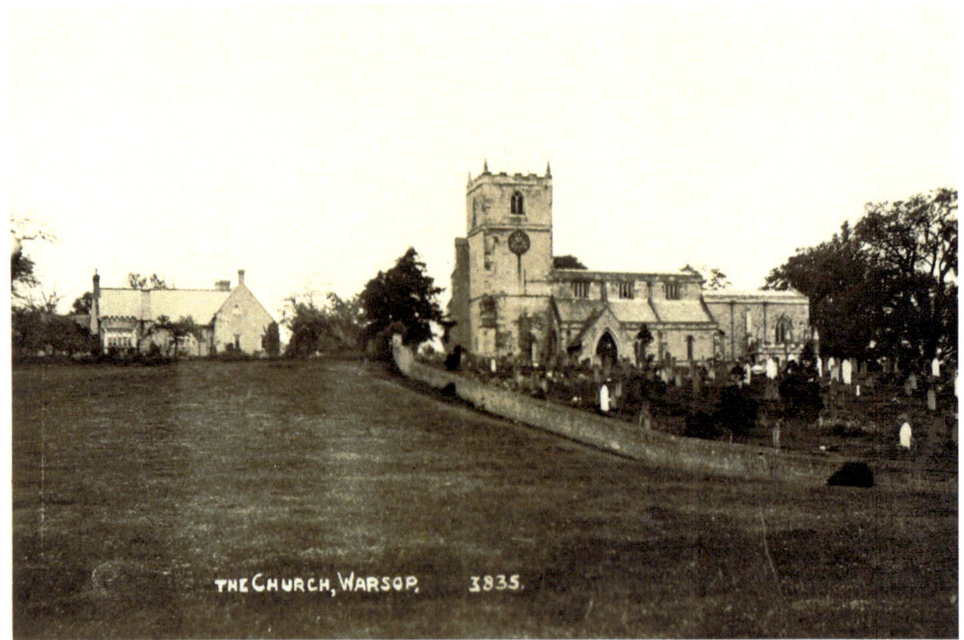

Harking back to pre-industrial times, the church at Warsop.

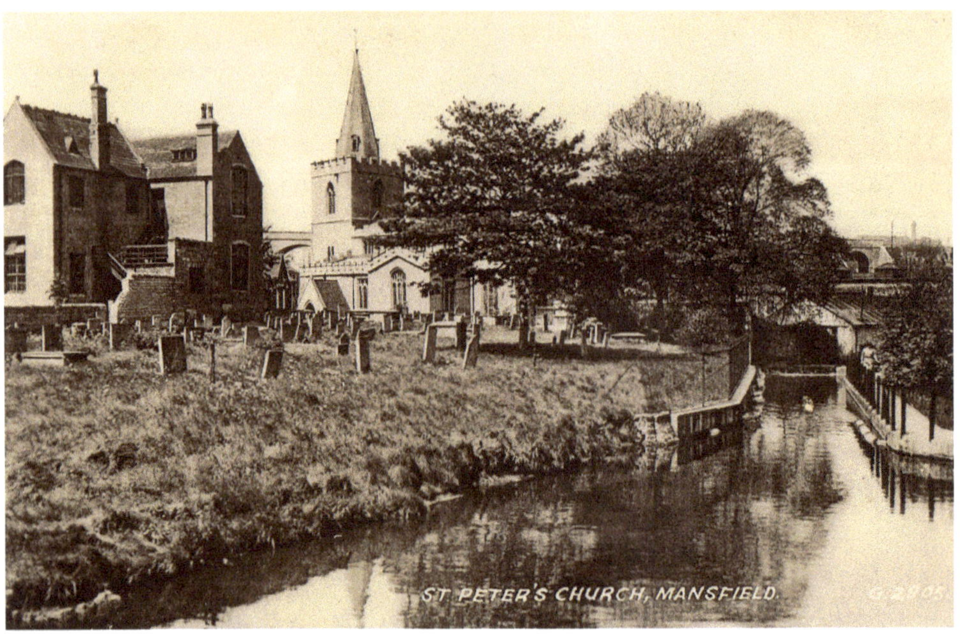

St Peter's church, Mansfield, in a pleasant rural setting.

3

SHERWOOD FOREST: HISTORY, MYTHS AND LEGENDS

The ancient trees, themselves rarities and home to amazingly rich biodiversity, are hugely important for conservation. However, the trees are also the stuff of history and legend. For visitors, they seem to be tangible evidence of the life and times of Robin Hood. In Sherwood Forest, history and Hollywood collide head-on, creating a place where reality and imagination infuse with one another to draw millions of tourists every year. Many of the old trees survive as a resource now recognised as being of global significance. For visitors, these iconic great oaks are timeless living connections with nature and with history.

For most people, Sherwood is inseparable from Robin Hood myths and legends. Indeed, the 'brands' of Robin Hood and the Major Oak must rate among the most powerful tourism icons in the world. Maybe the name derives from a generic term for an outlaw, 'Robin o' th' Woods', most likely not an Errol Flynn style character, but a down-market mugger. Nevertheless, the legend grew, and the main work about his life, *The Lyttle Geste of Robyn Hode*, was a printed book in 1495. Robin had an earlier appearance in literature in 1420, in Wyntoun's *Chronicle of Scotland*. It seems that the myths grew and merged into various earlier stories of Norman suppression and Saxon resistance, part-truth, part-fiction. By the seventeenth and eighteenth centuries, the folklore of Robin Hood had become popular, with several lays written about him and his band of 'Merry Men'. In early texts, the story is set in Yorkshire, and of course, everyone knows Robin hailed from Loxley, in Sheffield. Eminent South Yorkshire antiquarian Joseph Hunter suggested that the Robin figure was contemporary with Edward II (1284–1327), whereas *The True Tale of Robin Hood* (1632), gives Robin's death as somewhat earlier, on 18 November 1247, during the reign of Henry III. Interestingly, all these authors place Robin rather later than the popular time of the reign of King John (1199–1216), or a little earlier at the time of Richard I. For centuries, he has been a figure of popular resistance to overlord oppression; in some cases he is presented as a renegade noble, Robin of Loxley, the Earl of Huntingdon. Beyond this, the wider public knows Robin's henchmen such as Will Scarlet, Friar Tuck, and of course Little John.

Quite what the origins of the legend are is open to debate, but the use of the area as firstly a Royal Forest, and then a significant hunting palace and deer park, must be important. While the reality of Robin remains shadowy, the evidence for the palace, park and the hunt are real and tangible. The punitive laws also existed, though in most cases they extracted money rather than pain. Forest Laws created by King Canute in 1016 paved the way for the Forest

Laws of William the Conqueror (known as the 'Bastard' because of illegitimate birth, not his unpleasant nature) after the Norman Conquest. Canute set down how the animals were to be managed, so that a 'Hart Royal' was the term for a royal deer escaping into non-hunting land beyond the forest. Such a beast had to be captured and returned to the Royal Forest. Canute established the 'lespegend' to undertake three-yearly inspections of the Forests.

Around Sherwood, the terrain was wild and potentially hostile. Sir Ralph Plumpton, in lieu of his job of driving wolves out of Sherwood Forest, had lands at Mansfield Woodhouse known as 'Wolf Hunt Land'. Other animals of note in medieval landscapes were ubiquitous pigs; both wild boar for the hunt, and especially domesticated pigs of peasant commoners. In the autumn, the right of *pannage*, allowing pigs into the forest to gorge themselves on acorns, was hugely important to the local people. From Michaelmas to Martinmas, the forest would be thronged with people and pigs. Many fatted pigs were slaughtered and smoked or salted, or turned into sausages, with much kept for the long winter months.

King's Clipstone, King John's Palace & Deer Park

The first mention of a royal connection is in 1164, with £20 spent from the Honour of Tickhill (formerly owned by de Busli) for works on the King's Houses. This may have been the original construction or it could have been repairs to an earlier building. The King's Houses at this early time would be of timber not stone, and the expenditure reflected this. Indeed, before 1164, the main interest of the monarch in this area would have been the royal manor at Mansfield, a small, pleasant medieval town. In 1130, 40 shillings was spent to prepare a chamber for King Henry I.

The King's Houses were associated with the central location of Clipstone at the heart of the Royal Forest of Sherwood. In the medieval period, a 'Forest' was a clearly defined geographic area subject to Forest Law. The law protected the land to which it applied and this was generally open heath with large, open-grown oak trees. The Forest was not 'woodland' as we know it today, and might include in its boundaries entire villages, fields, commons, and coppice 'woods'.

The building provided royal accommodation plus facilities for the entourage and support, for feasting and the hunt itself. The size of the stables suggests the magnificence of the palace. In 1184, the keeper, Humphrey de Bussei, received 60 shillings to enclose the palace courtyard. By 1186, a new fishpond, the 'Great Pond of Clipstone', complete with dam, weirs and mill, was built close to the King's Houses.

From its origins as a Royal Hunting Preserve, this region was important for hunting, and the remains of King John's Hunting Palace bear testimony to this. The now much-fragmented ruins stand in an isolated plot near to 'King's Clipstone'. The Domesday Book (1086) notes a settlement here called 'Clipestune', then later 'Clipestone', 'Clippeston', or 'Clipiston'. The broken-down buildings are all that remain of a one-time substantial, medieval, royal palace, known as King John's Palace since at least the eighteenth century. It was previously called the 'King's Houses'. Although associated with King John, he actually spent little time here, perhaps only nine days. References to the King's Houses go back as far as 1164 and the reign of Henry II (1154–1189). The earliest building was between 1176 and 1180, with Henry ordering £500 spent here, and a deer park to be created at Clipstone. Hunting game was for royalty, aristocracy and senior clergy. Deer parks and the forest beyond provided recreation, food for great feasts, and a focus for the discussion of important issues of politics, finance and society. Reflecting this importance, in 1194, King Richard I chose this now isolated place to meet William, King of Scotland. Richard came to Clipstone on 29 March 1194, and again on 2 April, the second visit being to meet the Scottish king. This demonstrates that the buildings were sufficiently impressive for an important international conference. In 1290, Edward I convened his Parliament here.

The King's Houses were well appointed for the time, and today's ruins include remains from about 1180 of a Romanesque chamber with a large, buttressed, central doorway. A timber upper floor allowed views over the deer park from ornately carved windows. This was just one part of what became a large complex of buildings developed over a long period. We know there was a gatehouse, a tower, a separate hall and chambers for the king and queen, several chapels, kitchens, stables for 200 horses, and lodgings for many royal retainers. In addition, a great pond provided 100 pike and 1,600 roach during Edward II's visit in December 1315; these would be both food and sport.

In 1200, King John received 15 marks from the men of Mansfield for allowing them to resume their rights of common pasture in Clipstone Park. They had enjoyed these rights prior to the enclosure of the park by Henry II. The loss of traditional common and forest resources to local peasants was a recurring theme throughout the period, and these resources were vital to survival. However, it is interesting to see John, often vilified, negotiating a reasonable settlement. Nevertheless, the Forest Law and related matters were often ways in which the Crown might raise revenue, and the reality is that this was just such a situation. The theme was repeated during the reigns of Edward II and Edward III, when extensions to the park resulted in petitions from the men of Clipstone, Warsop and Mansfield Woodhouse. In this case, the complaints were over their loss of rights for 'housebote' (timber for building), haybote (timber for hedging), collection of ferns and leaves (for compost and manure), and over the right to pasture. In a rural society, these were the necessities of life.

Edward Longshanks, King Edward I, the 'Hammer of the Scots', carried out work on the Clipstone palace. For his visit in 1280, new chambers with chapels for the king and queen were built at a cost of £435 12*s* 6½*d*, and today's ruin may be the remains of this. Romanesque features suggest that at least some of the structure is dated earlier, perhaps to Henry II's developments in 1176 to 1180. However, in 1282, Edward I ordered the construction of a stable at the enormous cost of £104 8*s* 5*d*. This might take up to 200 horses, maybe the entire royal household, important when, in 1290, Edward hosted his Michaelmas Parliament here. This was a great gathering and accommodation at the King's Houses was so full that the clerks of the Chancery lodged at nearby Warsop.

Early maps of Sherwood Forest, particularly one from around 1400 found in the Belvoir Castle archives, show Clipstone Park clearly defined, circled by a paling fence. Place-names relate to the medieval park, for example 'ye pele' (i.e. Clipston Peel), 'Clipston ye dam' (the dam at the head of the Great Pond), and 'Clipston Parke'. Remarkably, because of the significance to the royal palace, the forest and the park, there is plenty of documentary and other evidence of the development and functioning of the estate.

Edward II frequently visited the King's Houses and while he did not noticeably alter the building, he extended the park. During the winter of 1316–17, Edward ordered the enclosure of 200 acres south-west of the park, and considered it necessary to build a peel, a fortified structure. The buildings included a great gate, two drawbridge windlasses, a ditch, hall, royal chamber, chapel, bakehouse, kitchen, barn and sheds for cattle, oxen and sheep. This reflected issues such as the need for more agricultural land during the early fourteenth century, and political problems, externally with Scotland and internally with Thomas, 2nd Earl of Lancaster.

Thomas was the eldest son of Edmund Crouchback, son of King Henry III and 1st Earl of Lancaster, and Blanche of Artois, Queen Dowager of Navarre. As one of the Lords Ordainers, Lancaster demanded the banishment of Edward's favourite advisor and, reputedly, lover, Piers Gaveston, and the establishment of a baronial oligarchy. With his private army, Lancaster helped separate the king and Gaveston, and was one of the 'judges' who convicted and executed Gaveston. In 1314, following humiliation and disaster at Bannockburn, Edward submitted to Lancaster, who became effectively the ruler of England for four years. However, despite his northern powerbase, Lancaster was unable to keep the Scots from raiding. In 1318, a new group of barons deposed Lancaster, who was then tried and executed. Because of his royal lineage, drawing and quartering followed by beheading was reduced to just beheading.

In January 1328, Edward III ordered Robert de Clipstone to dismantle the peel buildings except for the 'greater gate of the pele, and the house built over it', and to re-erect them at the King's Houses. However, during the early years of Edward III's reign there were numerous visits to the palace. Local commoners requested and negotiated the reallocation of rights back to before Edward II's expansion of the royal park. In 1340, Robert de Mauley was responsible for the manor and the park. The Clipstone and Warsop commoners gained consent to use the park's woodland resources in 1341, but the deer park was maintained.

By the mid-fourteenth century, the King's Houses at Clipstone were an extensive complex of palace buildings housing the overseers of the park and forest operations, and the residence of the king and royal court. The last reigning monarch to reside at Clipstone was Richard II. His successor Henry IV granted Clipstone Manor to George Dunbar, Earl of March (1338–1420), for life to compensate the loss of his Scottish lands on siding with the English against the Scots. The manor later reverted to the Crown and in 1434, Henry VI's council authorised £200 of repairs. In 1435–46, over £650 was spent on the King's Houses, including the building of a new tower. Then, in 1453, the manor was granted to the king's half-brothers, the earls of Richmond and Pembroke. When Edward IV came to the throne, the manor passed to George, Duke of Clarence, until he was executed in 1478, and Clipstone passed back to the Crown estate.

King's Clipstone was an important royal centre until late in the fifteenth century, by which time fashions and focus had shifted. By 1525, the King's Houses had fallen into disrepair and were described as 'ther is great dekay & ruyne in stone-work tymber lede and plaster'. Royal interest in the King's Houses and their park at Clipstone reduced, as was the case with such estates across the kingdom. The focus of kingly activities shifted to South East England, and the passion for deer hunting declined. Indeed, it was a general trend for the number of royal palaces and castles to reduce, while the size of the household rose, from about 120 in the reign of Henry I, to over 800 by the time of Henry VI. They required fewer but more splendid palaces, and the royal interest in Sherwood and Clipstone fell away. In 1525, this was reflected in a report entitled 'A survey of the dekayes of the manner of Clippeston':

First the southest end of the hie Chamber ther is in great dekay & ruyne in stonework tymber lede and plaster & the gavell ende of the same is flede outwarde so that a part of the rove and of flour of the said Chymber is fallen doune. Also ther was sume tyme begone a stone grees & yet is not fynyshed the which hath been the cause of the Ruyne of the said Chambre. Also the Chappell ther is in dekay and hath no cuverying upon it. Also the kechyn ther was new plasterid and the rof therof wantith poyntyng and amedyng of the slate, also on the said kechyn were ij chymnays begon and not fynishyd.

Interestingly, the survey only gave three buildings: a chamber, a chapel and a kitchen. If these really were the only structures remaining by 1525, then this is a remarkable decline and demolition in the 150 years following Edward III's repairs. By March 1568, a land grant referred to this being the 'site of the late castle', so we can assume major demolition.

In the fifteenth century, the landscape was also changing to a new function of ducal parks and great houses. By the sixteenth century, William Cambden wrote that Sherwood was 'much thinner' than earlier in its history. He suggested the decayed nature of the forest and that the cause was implicitly the fact that the forest 'feeds an infinite number of deer and stags'. This changed as ducal estates cut great swathes from Royal Forest and enclosed semi-feral red deer and fallow deer within sizeable parks – deer maintained for ornament, sport and the table.

Certainly, by the mid-eighteenth century the palace site was mostly stripped bare and left as the ruin we see today. To the casual observer today there is little to suggest the romantic and sometimes lavish history of the location. There are numerous houses across England with links to the early kings, and especially to King John and his passion for the chase, but this has a genuine claim to fame.

The soil of the area was generally not conducive to agriculture and this single factor above all others has protected the forest and heaths of Sherwood through the centuries. K. C. Edwards described this when writing in the twentieth century: 'The thin, poor soil, so loose in dry weather that the strong winds carry it from the fields in dust clouds does not encourage cultivation without special treatment. Vegetation is also somewhat impoverished by the dry conditions, resulting in a large amount of bracken and gorse, interspersed with oak and birch wood.'

Robert Murray Gilchrist, writing in the early 1900s, felt that the birch wood of Birklands 'was easily the finest in the British Isles'. Redfern notes how on sunny days in spring the sun permeates the forest, the silver haze merging with blue of the bluebells reflected in the silver-white bark of thousands of birch trees. Add to this the golden brown still showing from the bracken beds, and the heavy fragrance of a myriad of bluebell flowers, and the effect is a truly heady mix.

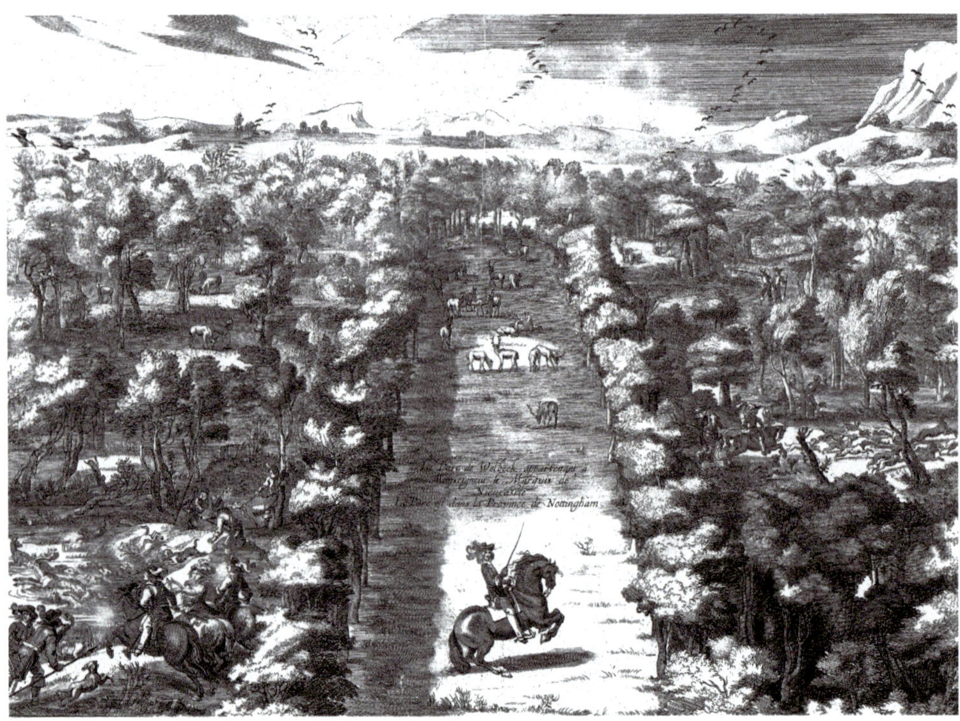

Copperplate engraving of Welbeck Park by Theodor Andreas van Kessel after Abraham van Diepenbeeck, 1737, showing the duke on horseback in the centre of the picture.

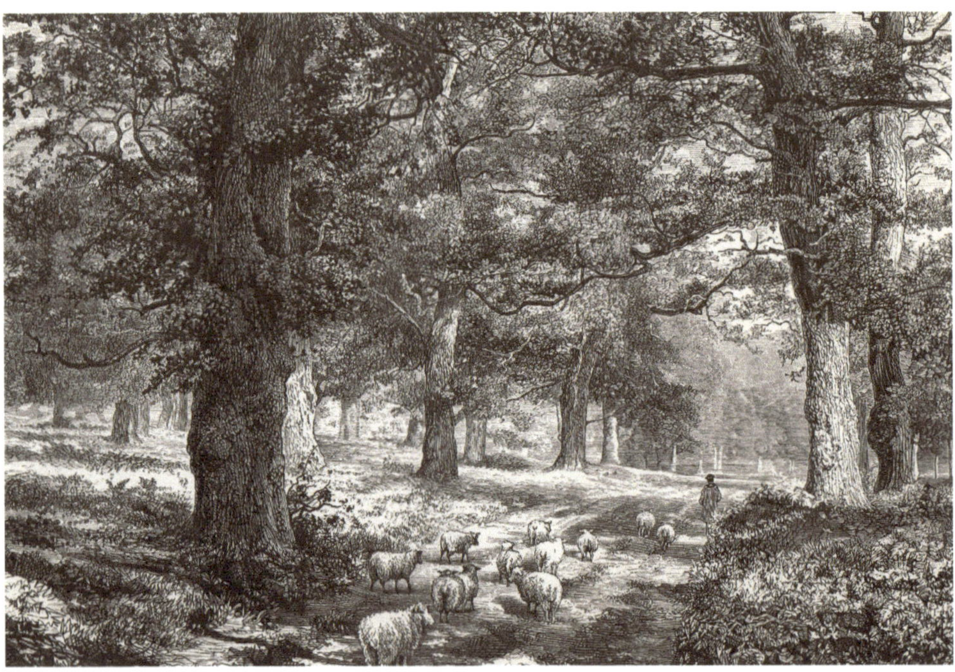

In Sherwood Forest – Victorian print showing the old oaks and a shepherd with his flock.

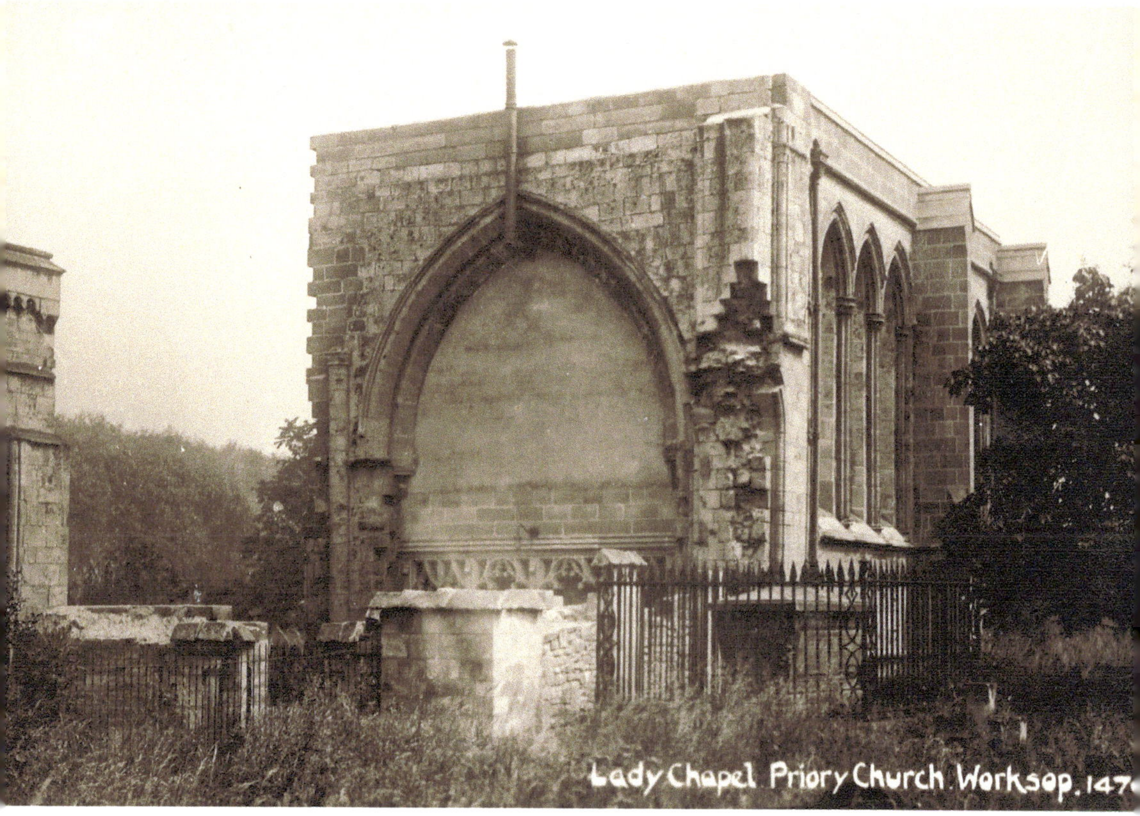

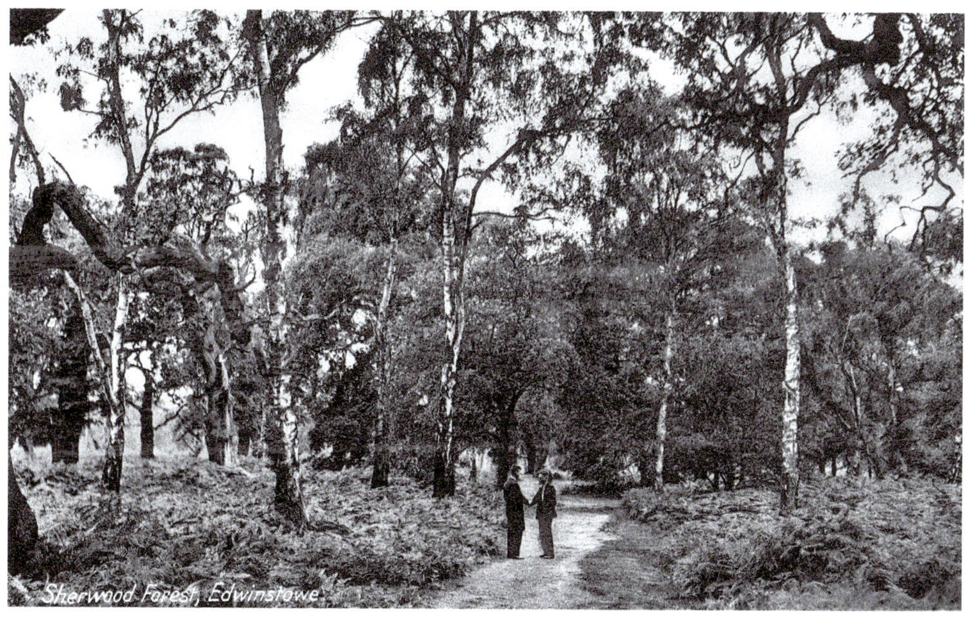

Above: Lady Chapel, Priory church, Worksop, 1920s.

Below: Sherwood Forest as a birchwood and heath, 1940s.

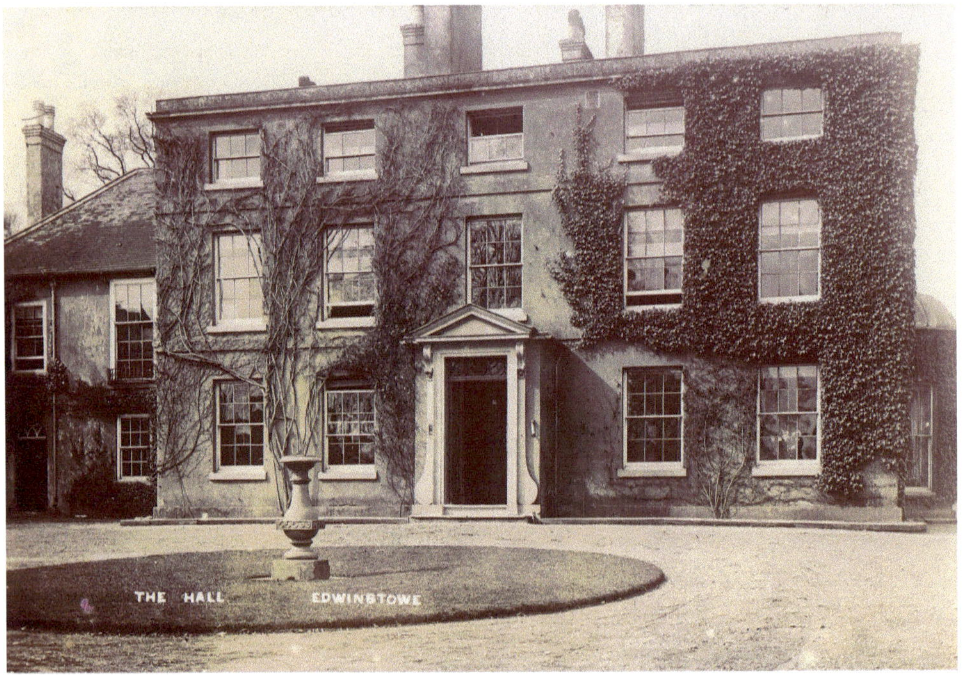

The Hall, Edwinstowe, early 1900s.

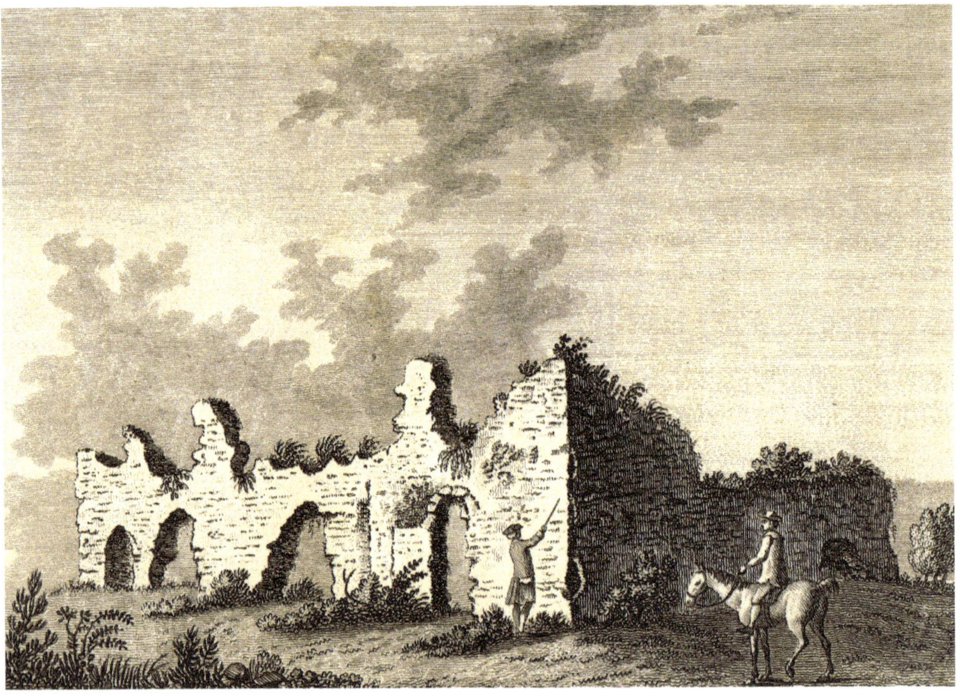

The King's House at Clipston shown in the late 1700s, a shadow of its former glory.

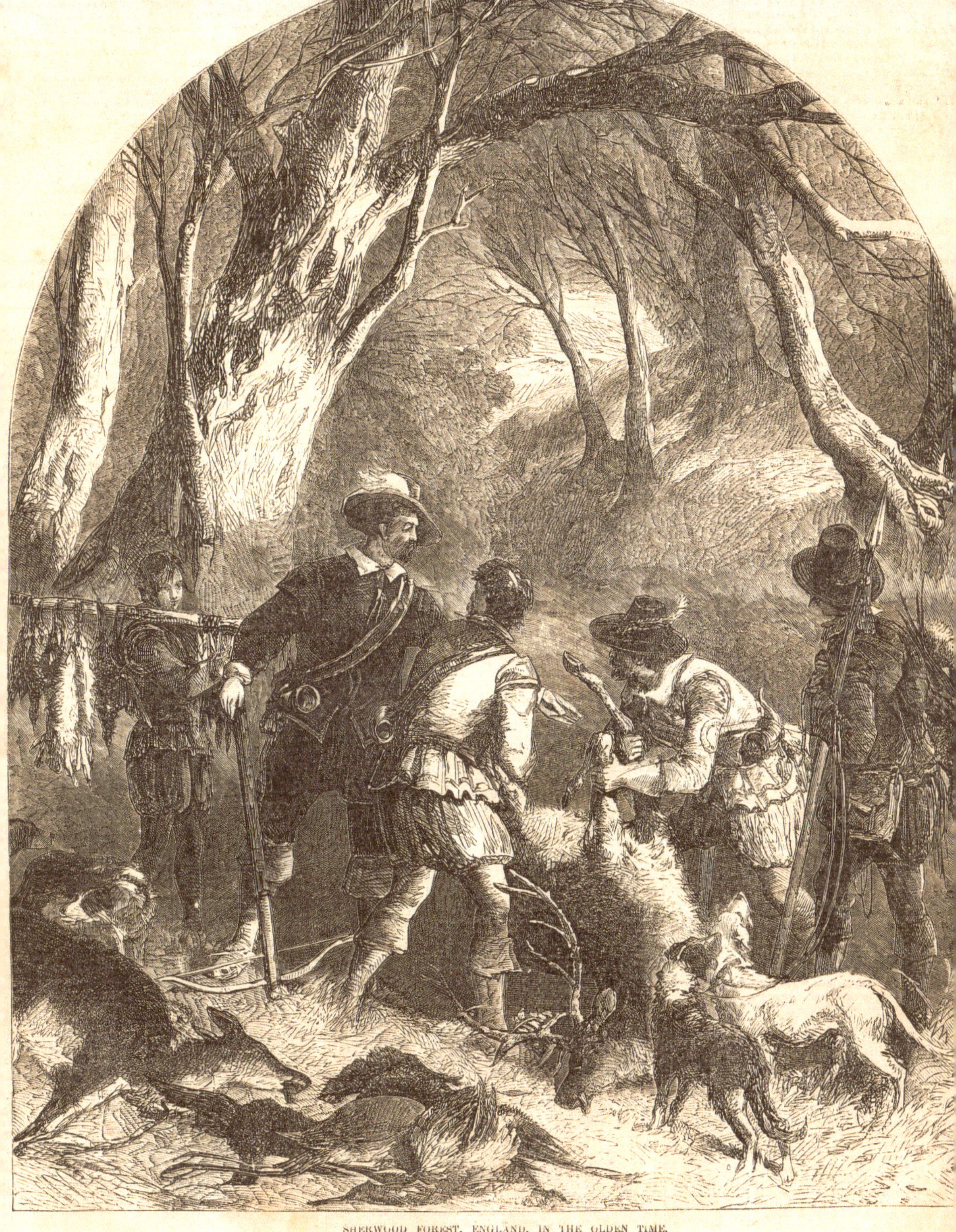

Sherwood Forest in the Olden Time.

4

THE REMARKABLE TREES OF SHERWOOD FOREST

At the core of the landscape and legends of Sherwood are great trees that characterised the medieval forest and the landscape parks. Now, often shrouded in planted conifers or re-grown birch, there are still pockets of wonderful veteran trees. Many survivors lost their tops, perhaps dramatically broken during an extreme ice storm in the 1700s. Other stag-headed specimens result from the falling water table due to extraction of groundwater.

Some 'lost' veterans have been 'haloed', to remove trees that threaten to choke them. However, sadly, the result is often accelerated death, as the ancient trees struggle to cope with the shock of changed microenvironment. The great oaks are mostly English oaks, *Quercus robur*, and a mix of trees managed as pollards, open-grown trees, and probably ones used as 'shreds'. There are ancient coppice trees but these are less obvious. Pollards were cut high to produce massed young re-growth for fuel or for small building work, but safely out of reach of grazing animals like cattle and deer. Shreds had side branches cut along the length of the main trunk, again for the same purposes. Coppice trees, protected from grazing in fenced or banked 'woods', were cut on regular cycles of fifteen to twenty-five years to produce poles of re-grown wood. These trees, each type managed differently over many centuries, were at the heart of the rural economy. Oak is said to live for nearly 1,000 years, around 300 in active growth, 300 or more at their peak, and a final 300 years or more in graceful decline. Routine cutting extends the life of trees beyond that of unmanaged specimens. A few mighty oaks, such as the Major Oak, are unmanaged 'open-grown' trees that originally dotted the wide-open heaths that dominated the Sherwood landscape. Because of their great stature, their twisted forms, and their obvious age, some of the Sherwood oaks have entered into folklore and myth, with several associated with Robin Hood.

The Major Oak
This notable tree was named after the antiquary Major Hayman Rooke, an eighteenth-century resident. The Major Oak is the single most popular visitor location in the forest, and probably the most famous and iconic tree in the world. By 1957, for example, the tree was receiving around 15,000 visitors on a Bank Holiday in August. Hayman Rooke, in 1790, published an account of the most notable oaks on the Welbeck Estate, and the Major Oak is over 30 feet in circumference and 60 feet in height. Back in the late twentieth century, hordes of pilgrims to the great tree could walk up, touch it, and even squeeze through a large gash in its side into its core.

Today, to conserve the roots from trampling, and the tree itself from prying tourists, there is a fence to keep people out. Wooden props support massive, low-slung branches, and cables hold the canopy together. The battle royal is on to save the tree from the ravages of time, although the trunk has been hollow for centuries. In the 1800s, the oak was called the Cockpen Tree because of fighting cocks, which roosted inside the hollow trunk. The tree has inspired writers for centuries, an example being Lord Tennyson, when after a visit to Sherwood, he wrote:

> Robin Hood: Where lies that cask of wine whereof we plundered the Norman Prelate?
> Little John: In that Oak where twelve can stand inside nor touch each other.

West of the Major Oak, stag-headed great trees dominate the Birklands. These are of both the species pedunculate and sessile, and the hybrids of the two.

Interestingly, in view of the legends and associations, when an oak was felled in the Birklands area in the late 1700s, Major Rooke discovered a brand-mark of King John, found about a foot from the centre of the trunk. Another tree revealed cut letters, and one a crown with W. M for William and Mary. This specimen was felled in 1785, and the letters were 9 inches from the outside of the bark and 3 feet 3 inches from the centre. One tree had 'I', which could be a 'J' for King John, 18 inches beneath the bark and 1 foot from the centre.

Simon Foster

One of the finest oak trees, called Simon Foster after a notable local villager, stood north-west of Edwinstowe. With commoner's rights, Foster herded his stock under the massive oak at night, and the tree acquired his name. The base was a great, spiral column, rising from a huge tangle of roots that spread over a wide area of ground.

The Centre Tree

Between Welbeck and Thoresby estates was significant landmark tree, which separated the two ownerships. The tree was only about 140 years old in 1900, a mere baby in comparison to the ancient veterans of the forest. Close by is the massive Archway Lodge built in 1844 by the 4th Duke of Portland. This mock version of the medieval gatehouse of Worksop Priory has the holy figures of the original replaced by carvings of Richard I, Robin Hood and his 'merry men'. From the Major Oak and Robin Hood's Larder, and around 80 yards wide, the Duke's Ride was cut to the Centre Oak and beyond.

The Shambles Oak or Robin Hood's Larder

Standing around a half mile from the Centre Oak was the Shambles Oak or Robin Hood's Larder. According to legend, Robin stored dried venison or other delicacies from the hunt in this tree. Sadly, at the time, the oak would have been too small, but it is a good story. However, inside the hollow tree there were iron hooks on which venison and other game were certainly hung. Unfortunately, sometime around 1913, a group of picnickers accidently set fire to the tree, and from then on it was described as 'something pathetic in the valiant greenness of its scanty leaves. It is like an old, old man who will be brave to the end'. The end came when, during a storm in 1961, after hanging on tenaciously for fifty years since the accident, the tree blew down.

The Duke's Walking Stick

One tree described by Major Rooke was the Duke's Walking Stick, a stunning specimen 111 feet tall, with a basal circumference of 14 feet. Mr Mearns, the estate gardener, suggested that the tree was felled just after the book on the Welbeck trees was published. At that time, it had a straight trunk, clear of branches to a height of 70 feet, topped by a small, rounded head of foliage, 'perhaps unmatched by any other in the kingdom for height and straightness'. When felled it produced 440 feet of solid timber and weighed 11 tons. Early in the 1900s, the Welbeck Estate was visited by Henry Elwes, and he was shown what he thought was the 'Walking Stick'. In fact, this was probably the 'Young Walking Stick', a similar but altogether smaller version of the original, and in Rooke's time only 95 feet high and 5 feet in circumference. To achieve the necessary size of the original the tree had to grow its girth by around 9 feet in 116 years.

The Seven Sisters Oak

East of the Great Lake at Welbeck there used to be a tree with seven trunks from one rootstock, and so presumably a very ancient coppice stool. Each trunk was about 90 feet high. The base was around 30 feet in circumference, but several of the stems blew down.

The Two Porters

These were two large oaks growing opposite each other at a gateway to Welbeck Park. One, measured in 1903, had a girth of around 25½ feet. The other tree was about 23 feet in circumference.

The Greendale Oak

As noted in the 1600s by the eminent writer on trees John Evelyn, this remarkable tree was reputedly bigger than the Major Oak at the same time. By the 1970s, the once magnificent tree was a shattered relic of its former glory, and all because of human vanity. In 1724, in an after-dinner wager, the Duke of Portland said he had a tree on his estate that could be cut to allow the passage of a coach and six horses. Once the wager was taken up by his guests, the duke proceeded to have the tree carved up. A hole, 6 feet 3 inches wide and 10 feet 3 inches high, was cut through the tree. The girth measured immediately above the top of this arch was 35 feet 3 inches. As well as cutting through the tree, the upper branches had to be removed in order to reduce the stress on the now much-reduced base. The wager was won by means of a purpose-built 'thin' coach and the skinniest horses available. Despite this devastation, the tree survived, though reduced in stature, and was still present, albeit as a hulk, in the 1970s. The countess had an oak cabinet made from the wood sliced from the venerable tree's heart. This item was inlaid with pictures of the tree plus the carriage and horses being driven through it.

Hayman Rooke considered the tree to be more than 700 years old in 1790, and in 1797, Throsby has stated it must be upwards of 1,500 years. It is sad to think how the tree would have lived several more centuries without the untimely intervention by the duke. As the now fatally injured tree fought to survive, it was planked up inside the cut to provide more support, and had chains put in place to hold its great branches. By the time Redfern was writing in 1974, he described it as 'a tumbled heap of seasoned timber, festooned still with old chains and monstrous supports', but he notes how the colossal stature of the original tree could still be appreciated.

The Pilgrim Oak

The writer Washington Irving paid a visit to the Pilgrim Oak outside the gates of Newstead Park, describing it as 'a venerable tree of great size, over-shadowing a wide area of the road. Under its shade the rustics of the neighbourhood have been accustomed to assemble on certain holidays and celebrate their ritual festivals.' It seems that the tree was under threat when the wicked Lord Byron set about destroying the estate, but the local people came to its rescue. They later presented it as a gift to the poet Lord Byron, and they benefited from the tree's shade for many more generations.

The Parliament Oak

Still present by the roadside, the Parliament Oak was originally on the boundary of Clipstone Park. Even by 1896, it was described as a senile wreck, and yet it bore a good crop of acorns. It is suggested that King John was hunting nearby when he heard of an uprising in Wales and in haste, called a Parliament together under the boughs of the great tree. The meeting under the great tree was on Peafield Lane, the ancient route between Edwinstowe and Mansfield Woodhouse. There is a similar story of a visit by Edward I on his way to Scotland, summoning Parliament at the same location. Even though much of the tree collapsed in the early 1900s, it had a girth of 29 feet. When Robert White of Worksop wrote about the tree in 1874, it he stated that 'what remains of it is only a shell in three or four parts, one of which is nearly round'. It is a sessile oak, and so is massive but not tall. Today it looks rather like an ancient coppice due to natural re-growth from the shattered base of the old tree. Protected by iron railings, the mix of old and new remains one of Sherwood's greatest trees.

The Shire Oak

Across the country are various 'Shire Oaks' at historic boundaries of English shires. Close by Whitwell Wood, in a field boundary where the counties of Yorkshire, Derbyshire and Nottinghamshire coalesce, is the 'Shire Oak' standing proudly in the hedgerow.

This short account covers the most famous of the great trees, but there are many others, less massive and less well known, for the visitor to discover for himself or herself. Furthermore, step into a wood such as Whitwell and you may find trees of even greater age than the Major Oak and its cousins. These are the ancient coppice trees such as small-leaved and large-leaved limes, reputedly well over a thousand years old, but that is a another story.

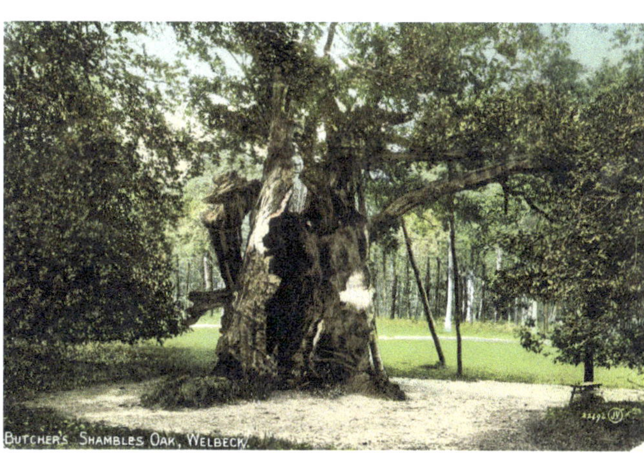

Butcher's Shambles Oak, Welbeck, early 1900s.

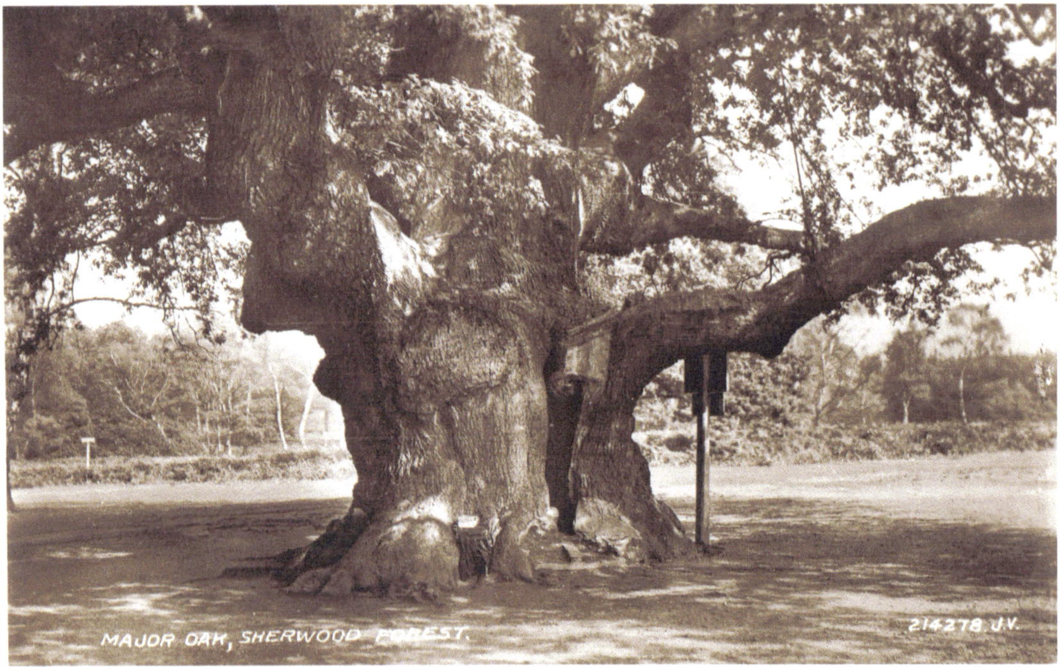

The Major Oak, 1940s.

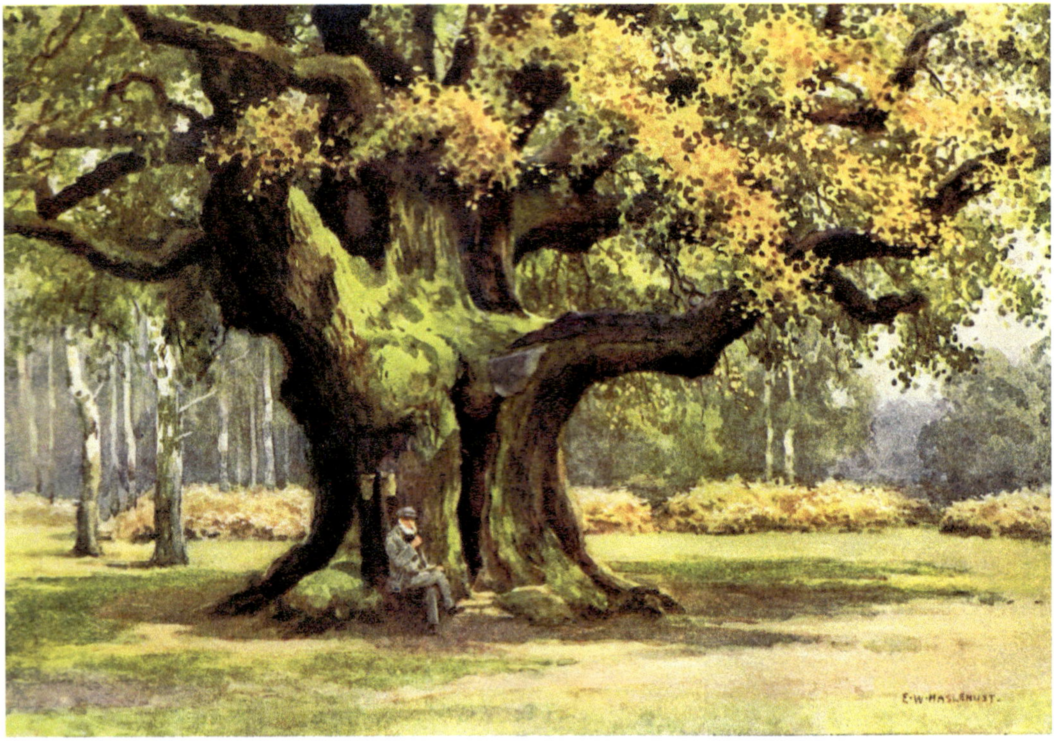

The Major Oak in the early 1900s.

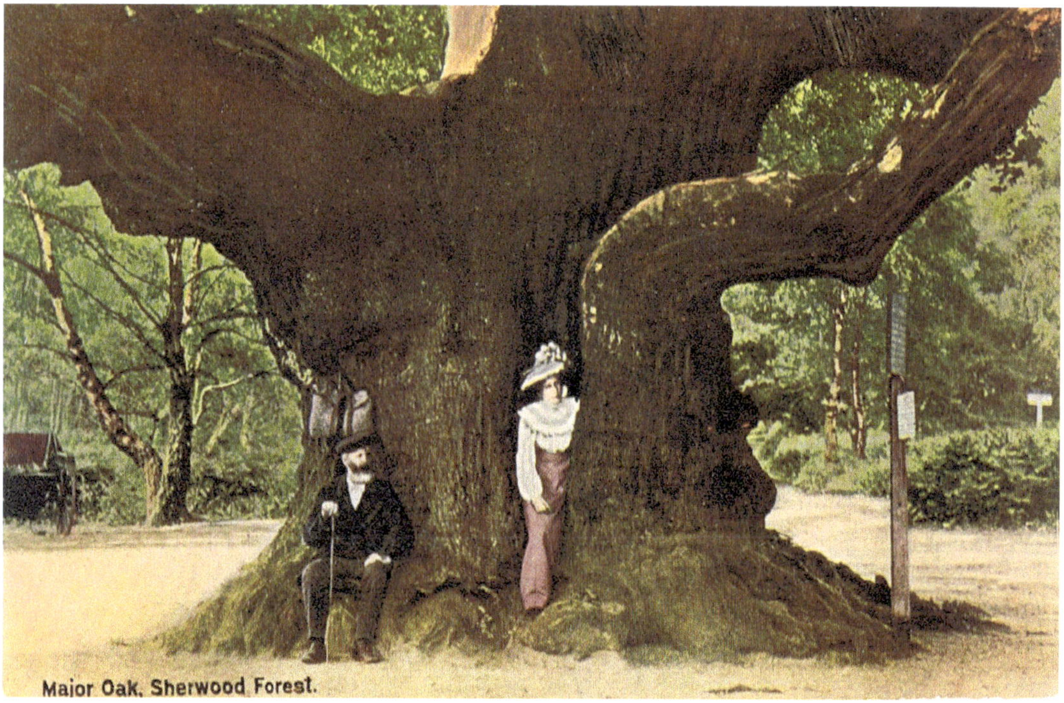

The Major Oak and visitors in the early 1900s, now with an explanatory sign.

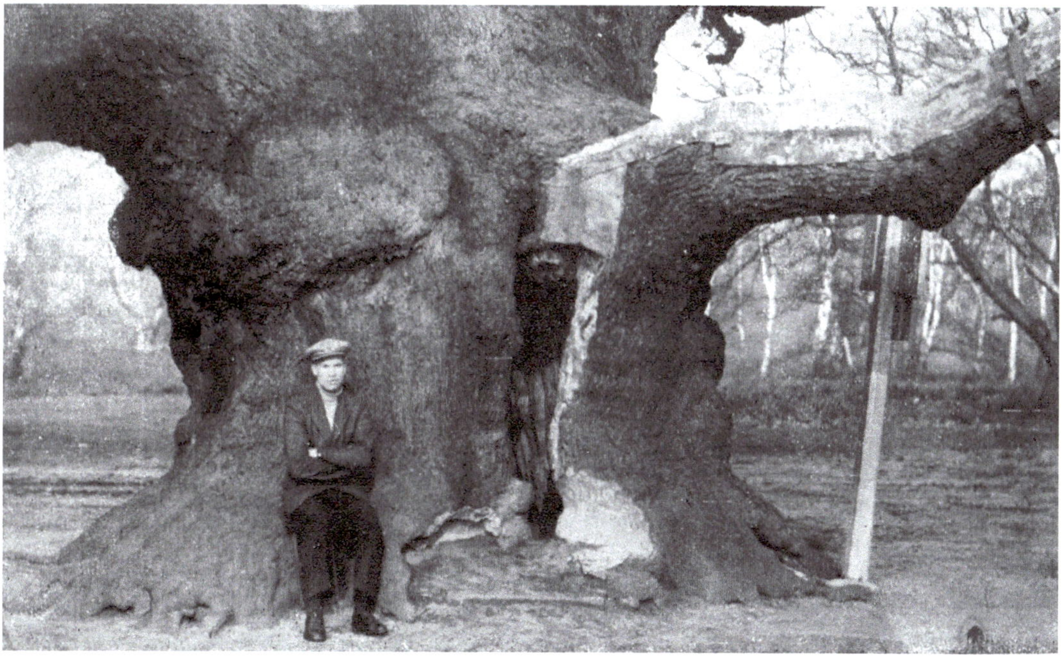

The Major Oak, early 1900s, described as aged 1,500 years, girth 35 feet, base 64 feet.

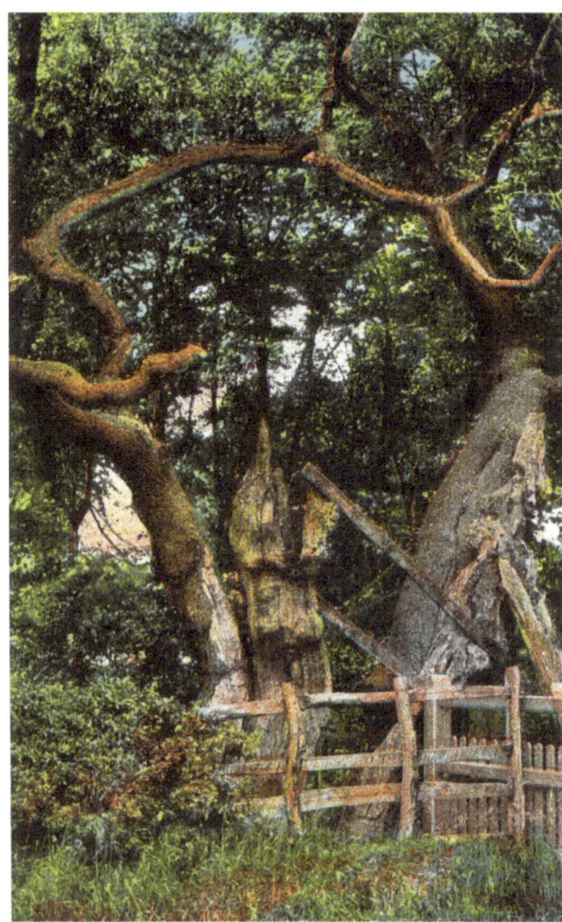

Left: The Parliament Oak, Mansfield, Nottingham, early 1900s.

Below: The Parliament Oak, 1905 postcard with some artistic embellishment.

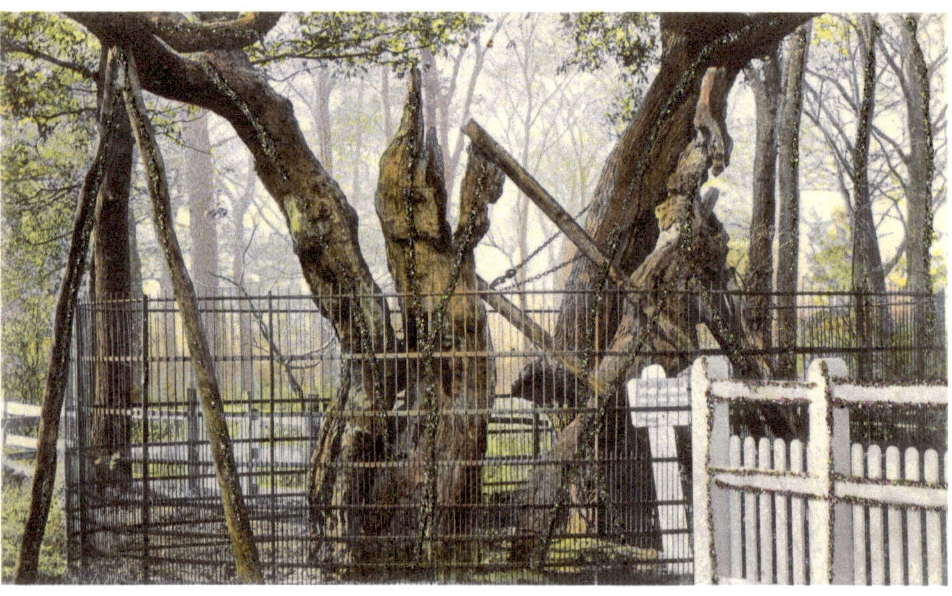

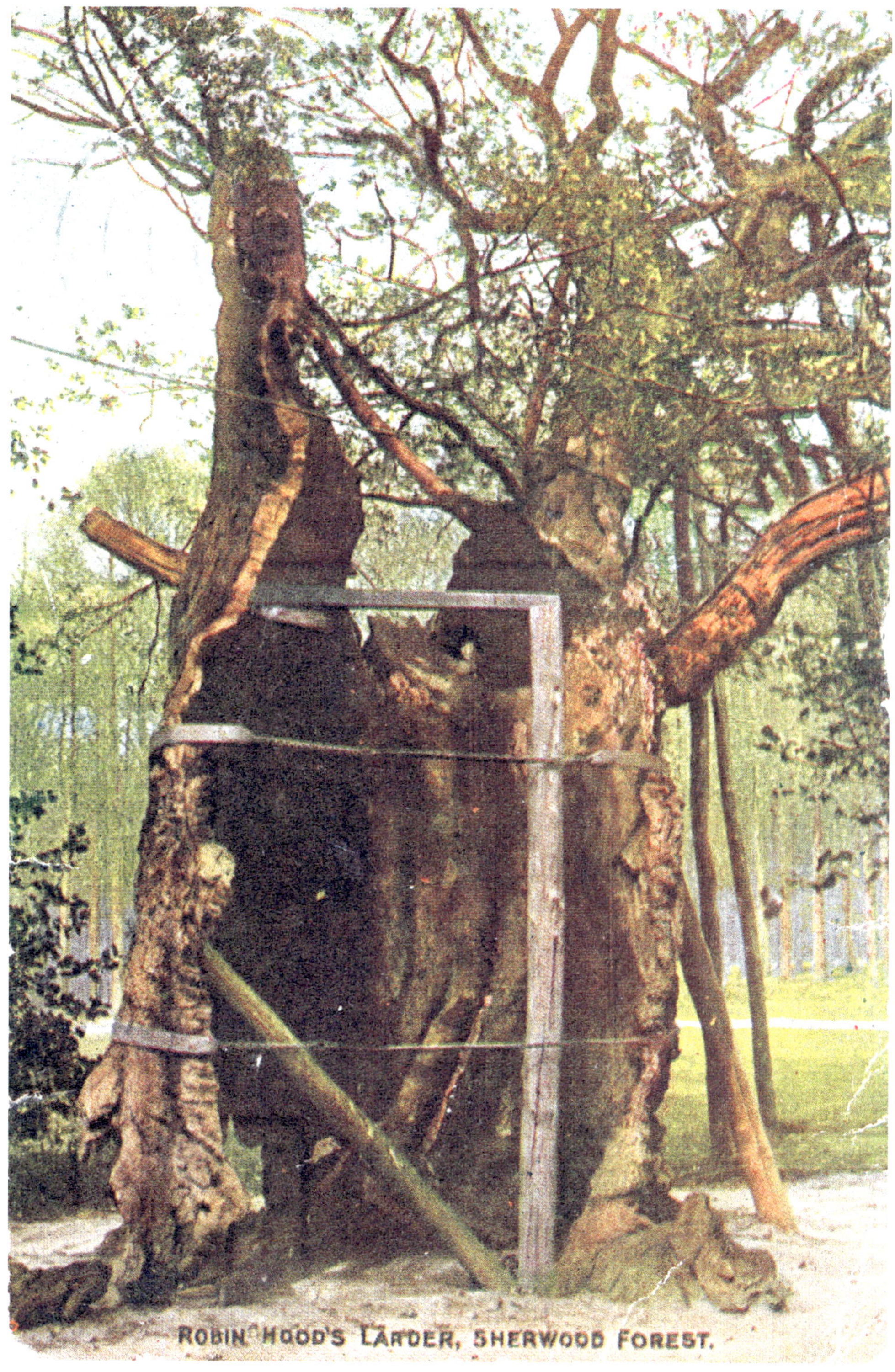

Robin Hood's Larder, Sherwood Forest, 1916, and a desperate attempt to hold it together.

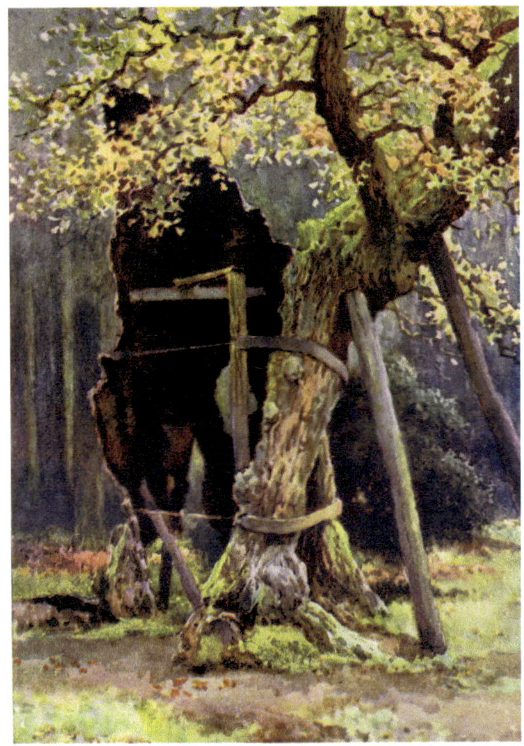

Robin Hood's Larder.

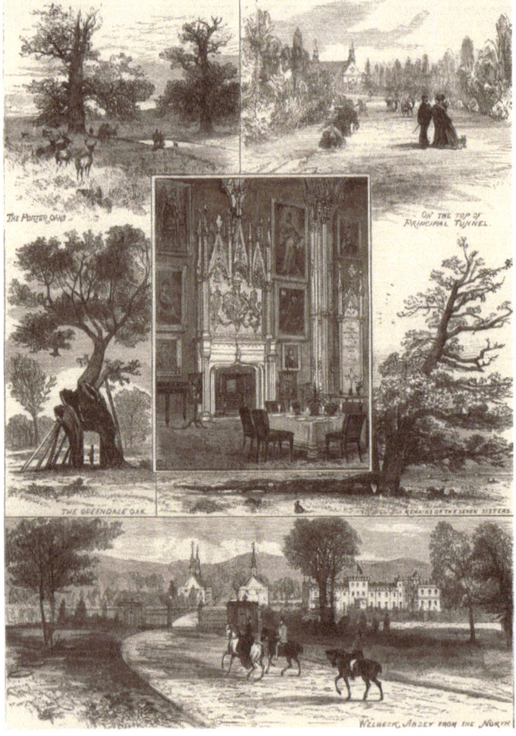

Welbeck and the oaks, 1881, from the *Illustrated London News*.

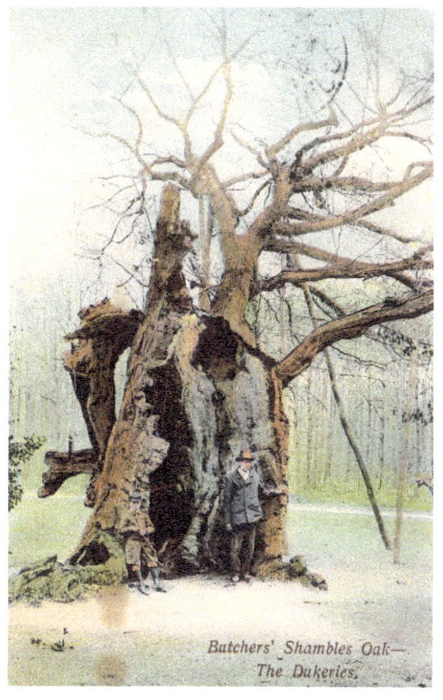

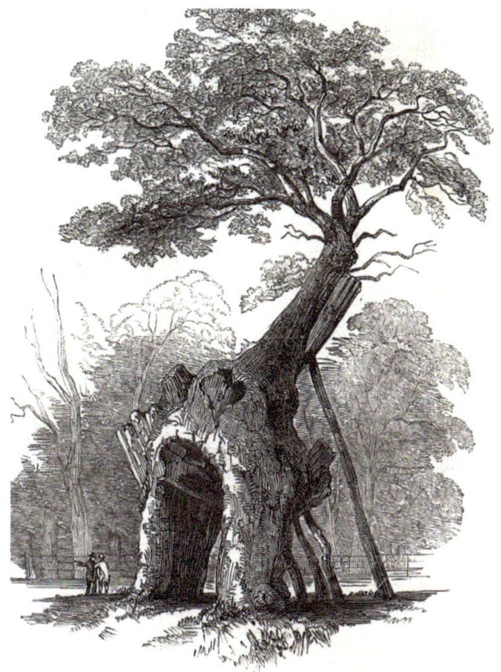

Above left: The Butcher's Shambles Oak, the Dukeries, early 1900s.

Above right: The Greendale Oak at Welbeck Park, 1848.

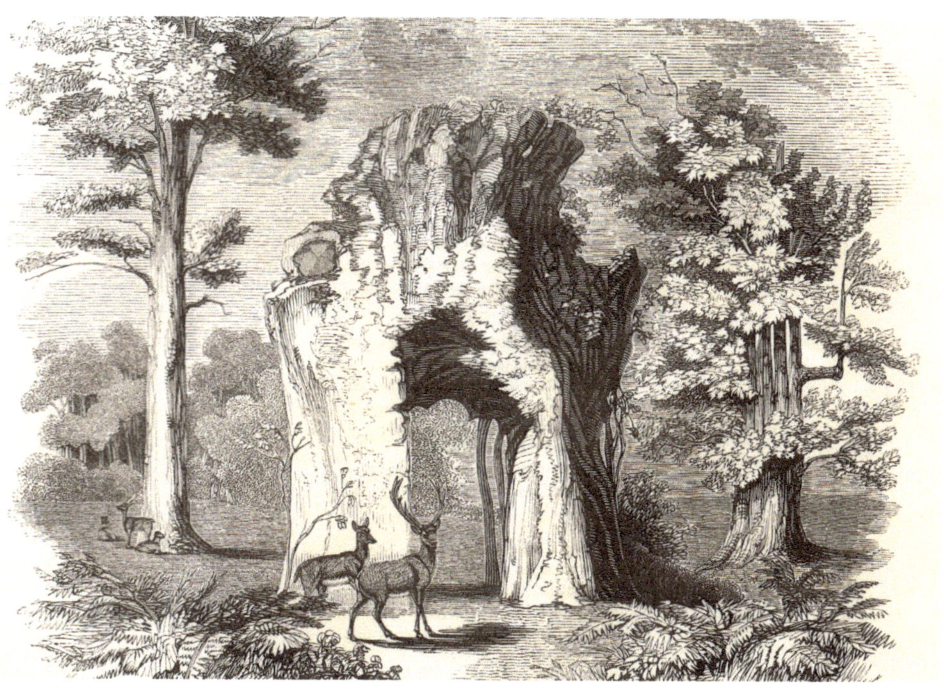

The Greendale Oak, the Seven Sisters and the Duke's Walking Sticks, from a Victorian print.

5

The Dukeries
and the Aristocracy

Central to an understanding of the Dukeries landscapes today is the history of the great halls and houses and their magnificent parks and estates. The Dukeries name was used since the eighteenth century and applied to a large tract of Nottinghamshire that once included grand estates of five dukes. Much of the surviving Sherwood Forest remains because it was encapsulated within the aristocratic domains. The five great estates today are Welbeck, Clumber, Thoresby, Worksop Manor, and Rufford, though the latter was never ducal. Along with these are smaller houses and halls, and sites such as Nottingham Castle and Wollaton Hall to the south, and Bolsover Castle and Hardwick Hall to the west.

The modern-day landscape includes estates still in private hands, exclusive prerogatives of dazzling wealth, and those owned by the nation, under the management of the National Trust and others, as the playground of millions. These sites and landscapes contain rich stories of ordinary people and of powerful and often eccentric aristocrats. More than anything else, these great estates have shaped the countryside and the places that we today call the 'Dukeries'. To visit the area today is to step back to another era and re-visit people and places long since forgotten.

It is worth considering for a moment the piece of legislation that had a pivotal impact on many of the great houses described. This was Henry VIII's Dissolution of the Monasteries. The actual legislation, because even Henry needed at least the appearance of law on his side, was the Suppression of Religious Houses Act 1535, or the Act for the Dissolution of the Lesser Monasteries. The main effect was to expropriate the lesser religious houses to the king. He

> shall have to him and to his heirs all and singular such monasteries, abbeys, and priories, which at any time within one year next before the making of this Act have been given and granted to his majesty by any abbot, prior, abbess, or prioress, under their convent seals, or that otherwise have been suppressed or dissolved … to have and to hold all and singular the premises, with all their rights, profits, jurisdictions, and commodities, unto the king's majesty, and his heirs and assigns for ever, to do and use therewith his and their own wills, to the pleasure of Almighty God, and to the honour and profit of this realm.

There was also retrospective regularisation of suppressions that had already taken place. The Act was only for lesser religious houses described as those 'which have not in lands, tenements, rents, tithes, portions, and other hereditaments, above the clear yearly value of two hundred pounds'.

The wording attacked such houses as 'dens of iniquity' and proposed that those in them should be 'committed to great and honourable monasteries of religion' and 'compelled to live religiously'. For the greater houses, their time was yet to come. The text makes fascinating reading, and seeks to justify closing monasteries and other religious houses because of their disreputable living. There was probably some justification, with some religious houses even running quite profitable brothels, but really, the intention was to take over resources. The preamble to the Act is as follows:

FORASMUCH as manifest sin, vicious, carnal and abominable living is daily used and committed among the little and small abbeys, priories, and other religious houses of monks, canons, and nuns, where the congregation of such religious persons is under the number of twelve persons, whereby the governors of such religious houses, and their convent, spoil, destroy, consume, and utterly waste, as well their churches, monasteries, priories, principal houses, farms, granges, lands, tenements, and hereditaments, as the ornaments of their churches, and their goods and chattels, to the high displeasure of Almighty God, slander of good religion, and to the great infamy of the king's highness and the realm, if redress should not be had thereof. And albeit that many continual visitations hath been heretofore had, by the space of two hundred years and more, for an honest and charitable reformation of such unthrifty, carnal, and abominable living, yet nevertheless little or none amendment is hitherto had, but their vicious living shamelessly increases and augments, and by a cursed custom so rooted and infected, that a great multitude of the religious persons in such small houses do rather choose to rove abroad in apostasy, than to conform themselves to the observation of good religion; so that without such small houses be utterly suppressed, and the religious persons therein committed to great and honourable monasteries of religion in this realm, where they may be compelled to live religiously, for reformation of their lives, there can else be no redress nor reformation in that behalf.

This began the transfer of land, wealth and resources from Church to Crown and aristocracy. Indeed, many families who became wealthy on the back of the Dissolution remain so today. The impact on the Sherwood region was radical, and a major factor in shaping the landscape from then onwards.

Worksop Manor

This is no longer a great ducal residence, but remains a modestly imposing country house. The earlier dwelling was grander, and a property of the dukes of Norfolk, with a Saxon lord dispossessed by an imposed Norman overlord, Roger de Busli, a favoured companion of William the Conqueror. His estates extended far to the north to include the lands of Hallamshire, now Sheffield. Eventually the lands passed to various sub-tenants, with Worksop and Hallamshire owned by the de Lovetots. Matilda de Lovetot, born in AD 1174, inherited the estate and married Gerard de Furnival. Gerard was a knight crusader and reputedly brought back to Britain the Cedar of Lebanon, the descendants of which are seen at Worksop and nearby Clumber. Thomas de Furnival was made baron in 1294, the peerage continuing to modern times, though in abeyance after the death of the nineteenth baroness. The estates were expanded as Maud, Baroness Furnival, married the wealthy Sir John Talbot, a highly regarded soldier and captain of English forces during the Hundred Years' War (1337–1453). Talbot was celebrated by Shakespeare as 'Valiant Talbot … hundreds he sent to Hell and none durst stand him'. He rose to become Earl of Shrewsbury, but his luck ran out and he died in battle in 1453, the last year of the war.

As with other ducal estates, the Dissolution of the Monasteries provided opportunities to expand and consolidate. The 5th Earl acquired the lands of Worksop Priory via a transaction and exchange with Henry VIII who wanted their estate at Farnham Royal. Attached to the latter was the tradition of providing the Coronation glove to the new monarch, the service subsequently transferring to the priory lands at Worksop Manor. By 1859, the estate passed from the Duke of Norfolk to the 5th Duke of Newcastle, and the traditional right ultimately became the responsibility of the trustees of the 9th Duke. However, at the last Coronation, the right, vested now in a limited company, was unfulfilled.

In Elizabethan England, the 6th Earl of Shrewsbury had the onerous duty of being responsible for the imprisonment and guardianship of Mary, Queen of Scots. He was also the fourth husband of Bess of Hardwick, thus joining the lines of another two great families. Mary spent much of her imprisonment at the manor house of Shrewsbury's estate in the then small town of Sheffield, and at Chatsworth House in the Peak District. When Lady Alathea Talbot, the daughter of the 7th Earl of Shrewsbury, married Thomas, the Earl of Arundel and grandfather of the 5th Duke of Norfolk, the estates passed on again, this time to the powerful Howards of North Yorkshire.

Worksop Manor remained an important seat throughout the time from the Tudors onwards, a strategic gateway between the North and the South. On his journey south, to be crowned King James I of England, James VI of Scotland was entertained there by the 7th Earl of Shrewsbury. Charles I was another visitor. Until a tragic fire in 1761 burnt the house to the ground, with more than 500 rooms, the manor house was one of the largest buildings in Tudor England. Lost to the fire was more than £100,000 in artworks alone, at the time a vast fortune. Having no children, the 9th Duke of Norfolk decided to re-build the house for his nephew Thomas, and when he died unexpectedly in 1763, his half-brother Edward became the heir. The new design was to be in the Palladian style, overseen by James Paine, and when the new north wing was completed there were great celebrations. However, tragedy struck once more and Edward, stricken by measles, died. Further building work ceased, and what might have been one of the greatest privately owned houses in all of Europe remained as just the north wing. Even this was as large as many large country properties. Later, dukes of Norfolk concentrated their energies on estates elsewhere and Worksop slowly declined, unfinished and uninhabited. Then, in 1839, at a price of £370,000, the Worksop Manor Estate became another acquisition of the 4th Duke of Newcastle-under-Lyme. He purchased the estate from the Duke of Norfolk as part of his consolidation of family estates in Nottinghamshire. However, the Newcastle ownership of the property lasted under fifty years. The Newcastles did not need another family seat so close to Clumber, and the duke, having financial difficulties, demolished the north wing. Existing staff accommodation was converted into a modest country residence and in 1890, together with surrounding parkland, was sold to Sir John Robinson, a breeder of thoroughbred horses. Much of the remainder of the estate was disposed of in individual lots. Sir John's great-nephew, Captain John Farr, succeeded him and the estate, though not the lordship, which remained with the family.

Clumber Park

Arriving at Clumber through any of the main entrances involves passage through an impressive gateway. The classical design of the Apleyhead Lodge off the A614 is especially

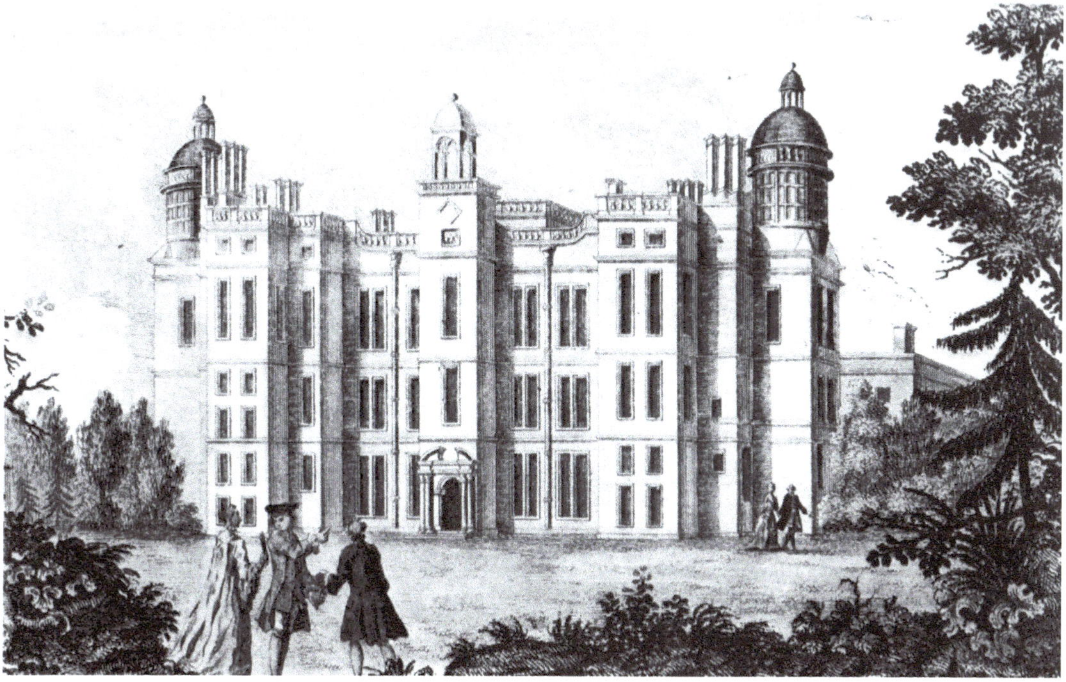

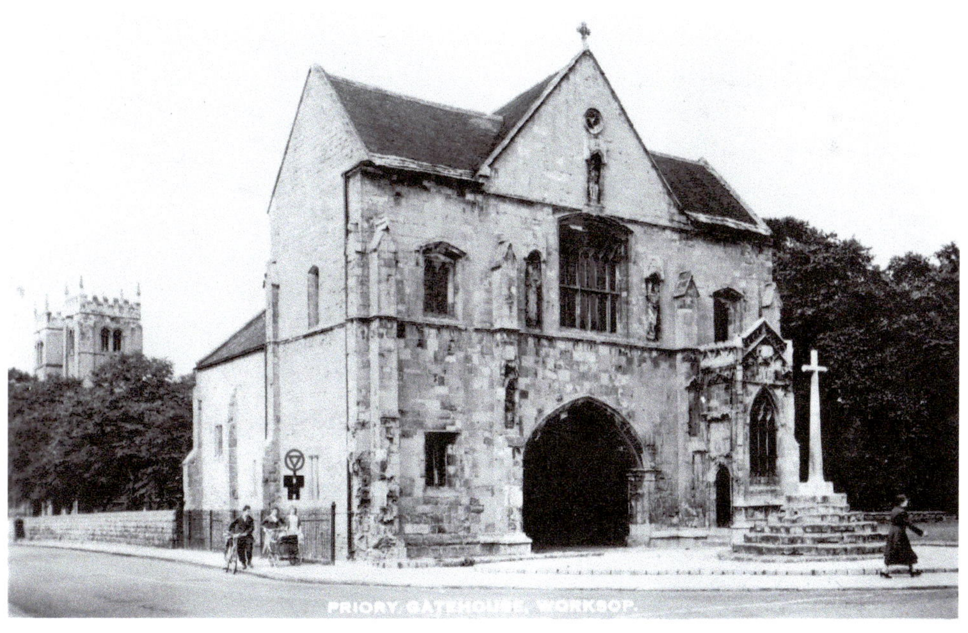

Old Worksop Manor as a stunning building before the fire of 1761.

The remarkable Priory Gatehouse, Worksop, 1971.

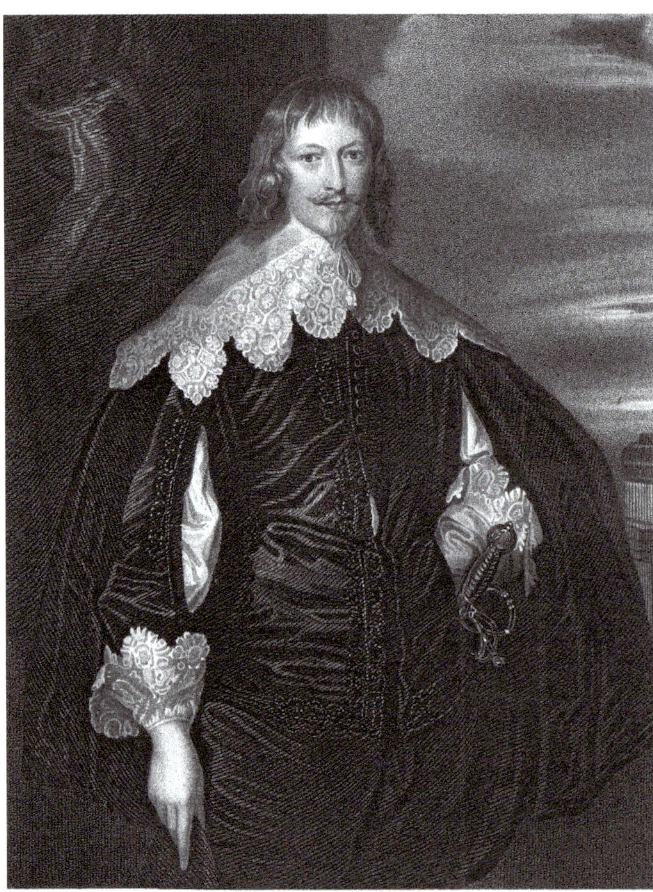

Left: William Cavendish,
Duke of Newcastle, by
Vandyke, born 1592.

Below: Worksop Manor.

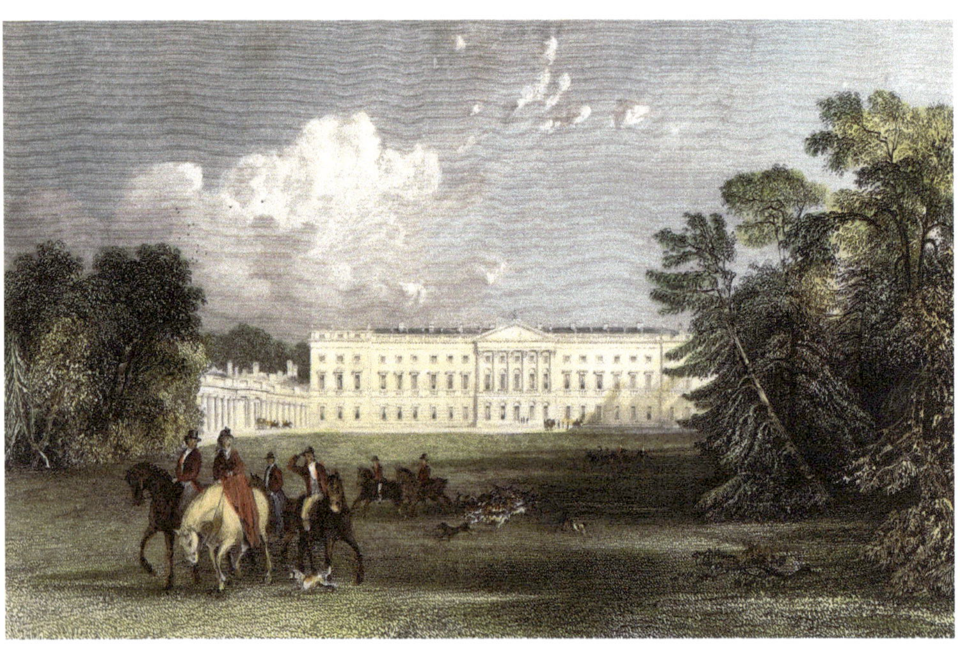

impressive and the 3-mile-long Duke's Drive, boasting the finest double-rowed lime avenue in Europe, forms a dramatic entrance. The slight anti-climax at Clumber is due to the lack of a major house at the end of the splendid drives. However, with National Trust's restoration of the remaining buildings, and of course the large private church of the estate, there is plenty to see and enjoy.

In 1707, by royal warrant from Queen Anne, John Holles, 4th Earl of Clare and 3rd Duke of Newcastle-upon-Tyne, first enclosed Clumber as a deer park. At this point, the main seat of the Holles was Haughton, a rather imposing country seat with landscaped grounds and formal gardens. Long since lost, some of the estate was included within the enclosure of Clumber Park. At the time, Clumber was described as 'a black heath full of rabbits, having a narrow river running through it, with a small boggy close or two'.

Thus began its association with the Newcastle title, something complicated by links to both 'upon-Tyne' and 'under-Lyme'. The estate only emerged as a significant family seat in the later eighteenth century. This development into a grand house and park began with Thomas Pelham-Holles, 1st Duke of Newcastle-under-Lyme, when he built a mansion house on the site. While ostensibly in the name of the 1st Duke, much of the work was overseen by his nephew, Henry, 9th Earl of Lincoln, and he inherited the title of 2nd Duke of Newcastle-under-Lyme. Henry decided to build at Clumber in 1770, abandoning the old family seat at Haughton. Stephen Wright, also responsible for the ornamental bridge, the temple folly and the lodges, designed the house. In the 1790s, the lake was described as having 'proud chested swans sailing gently', very different from the small stream and its boggy heath.

The 1st Duke of Newcastle-upon-Tyne, of the second creation, John Holles, Earl of Clare, died without a male heir, and so a short-lived dukedom became extinct. Leaving his Welbeck estates to his daughter Henrietta, Clumber passed to his adopted heir, Thomas Pelham. Thomas took the family name Pelham-Holles, and four years on, was granted the dukedom of Newcastle-Upon-Tyne of the third creation. The 1st Duke of the third creation was no more successful in producing a male child than his predecessors, but to safeguard the title he was granted a second dukedom, this time of Newcastle-under-Lyme. The clever ruse was to allow this to pass to his nephew Henry Fiennes-Clinton, thus keeping the line alive. Henry was already 9th Earl of Lincoln. The Newcastle-upon-Tyne title became extinct again, and the twentieth-century dukes descended through this line.

The 4th Duke of Newcastle-under-Lyme, apparently a highly regarded, and for the times, humane man, became the target of severe animosity from radical groups. A high Tory, he was against social and political changes, and especially the Reform Bill. Consequently, he was viewed as a manifestation of Tory reaction and of the deeply embedded privilege that such society implied. As a result of his high profile and entrenched views, in October 1832, an irate mob attacked his house in Nottingham, Nottingham Castle, and burnt it to the ground. In London, the rioters stoned the duke's house in Portman Square, although by the time they arrived, it had been fortified sufficiently to more or less protect it. When he died in 1851, the estate was in financial difficulties as the duke had over-extended his resources in the purchase of Worksop Manor. He was buried with his wife the duchess in the mausoleum he built at Markham Clinton near Newark. Completed in 1833, this splendid classical building with its domed tower and with stunning marble effigies was designed by Sir Robert Smirke as a mausoleum for the duchess.

The late duke's son inherited the estate to become the 5th Duke. Although a tireless public servant, he was deeply unpopular as Secretary of State for War during the Crimean crisis. Working long hours every day to try, unsuccessfully, to reform the War Office, the job took its toll on his health and he resigned due to public antagonism. However, for the estate and for us today, there was a bonus in his retirement from public office. It was then that he planned and planted the lime tree avenue at Clumber. The duke briefly served as Colonial Secretary in 1859 but, suffering from ill health, he returned to Clumber where, in 1864, he died sat in his chair.

The 6th Duke died in February 1879, and a month later, much of the house was badly damaged by fire. This was something that major houses had been vulnerable to ever since the Middle Ages. Twenty or more rooms were affected, and the 7th Duke, while still a minor, set about restoration and improvement. He called upon the son of Sir Charles Barry, the architect formerly involved with Clumber, to undertake the necessary works. The late Victorian house was a splendid affair with richly decorated rooms and a state dining room for 150 guests. The grand hall, 82 feet by 45 feet, and other rooms were hung with paintings by famous artists and adorned with statues by famous sculptors. A major feature was the massive marble chimney piece in the study. The church, designed by distinguished Victorian architect G. F. Bodley R. A., was built for the 7th Duke of Newcastle in 1884.

Guests could descend the steps of the terraces to the lakeside to see the miniature, fully rigged ship *The Lincoln* at its moorings. On special occasions, they might also bombard the same boat with cannon fired from the shoreline, an image of English aristocratic decadence.

However, from the 1890s to the 1930s, a tidal wave of change swept through the English landscape. Political, social and economic reforms and changes led to rapid declines in great country estates.

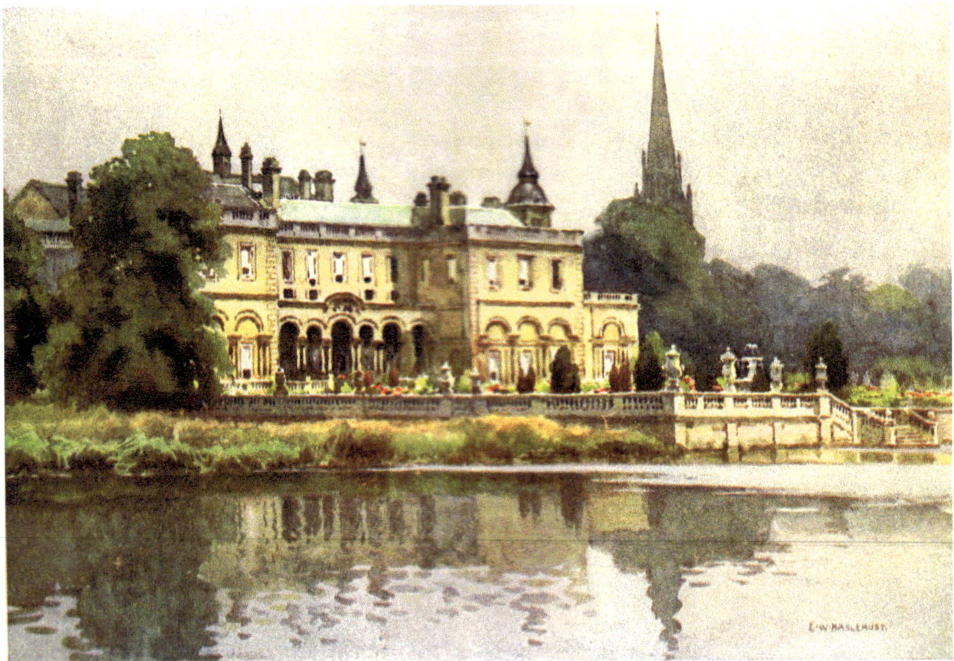

The house and church at Clumber.

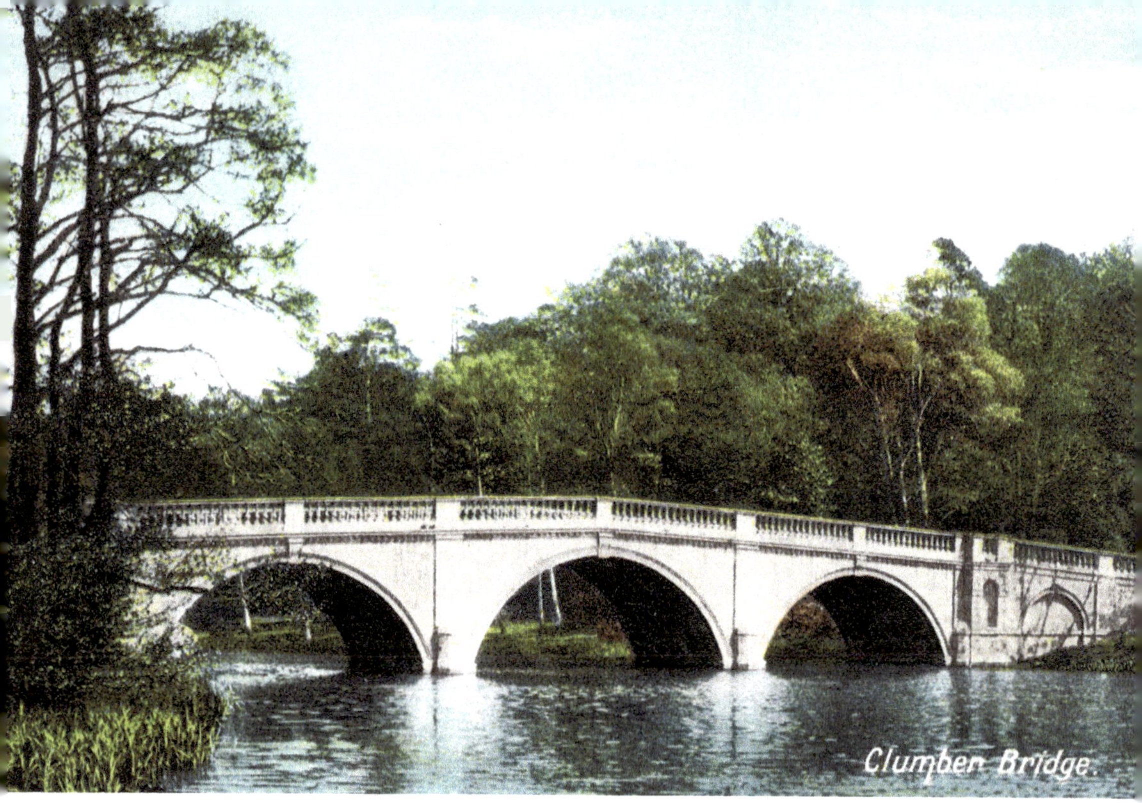

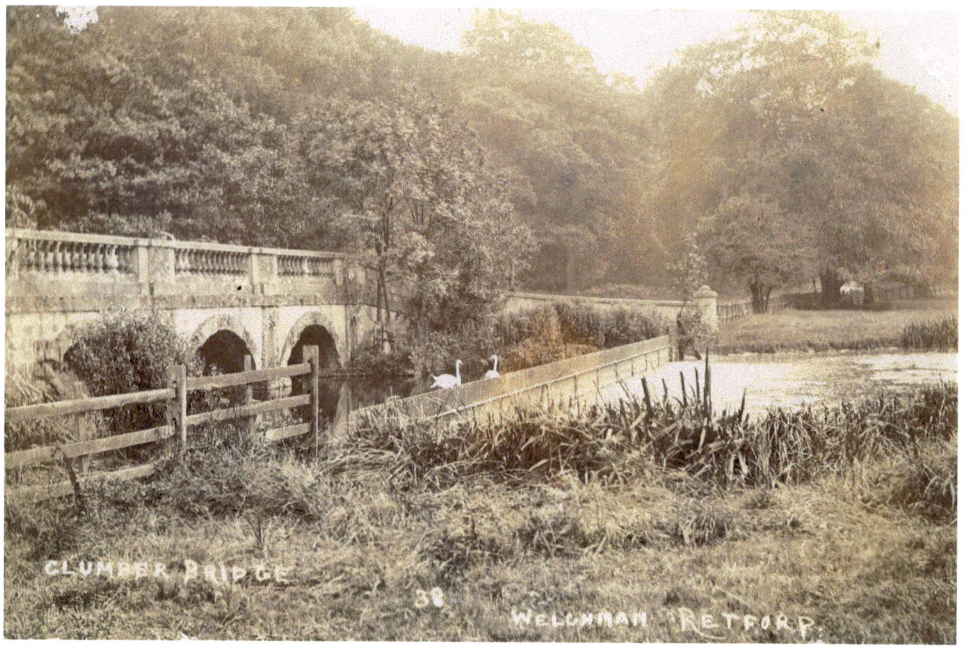

Clumber Bridge, still a favourite feature of the estate for visitors, in the early 1900s.

Clumber Bridge, early 1900s, with swans and a barrier across the river.

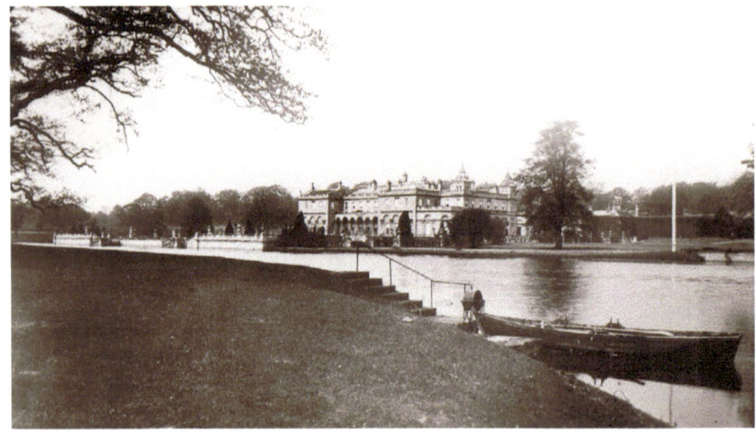

Clumber House
south lawn and
moored boat, 1915.

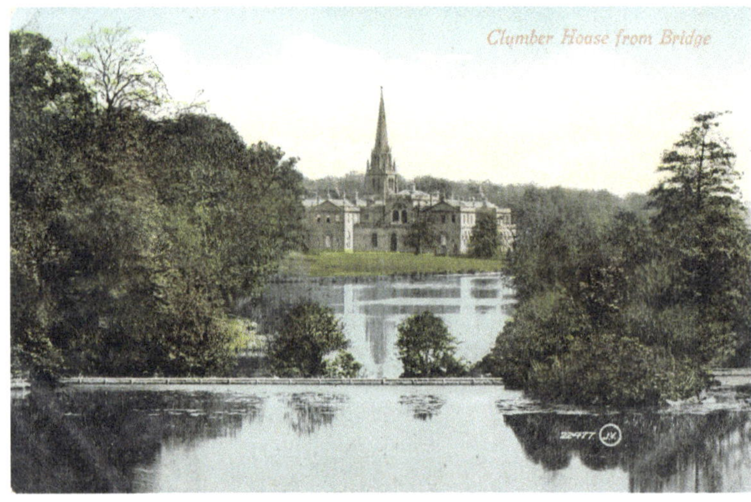

Clumber House
and church from
the bridge, 1912.

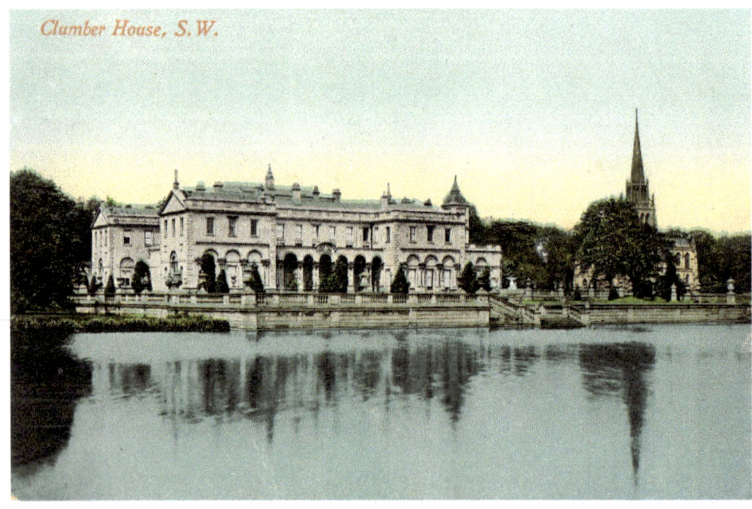

A lost treasure
– Clumber House
from the south-
west.

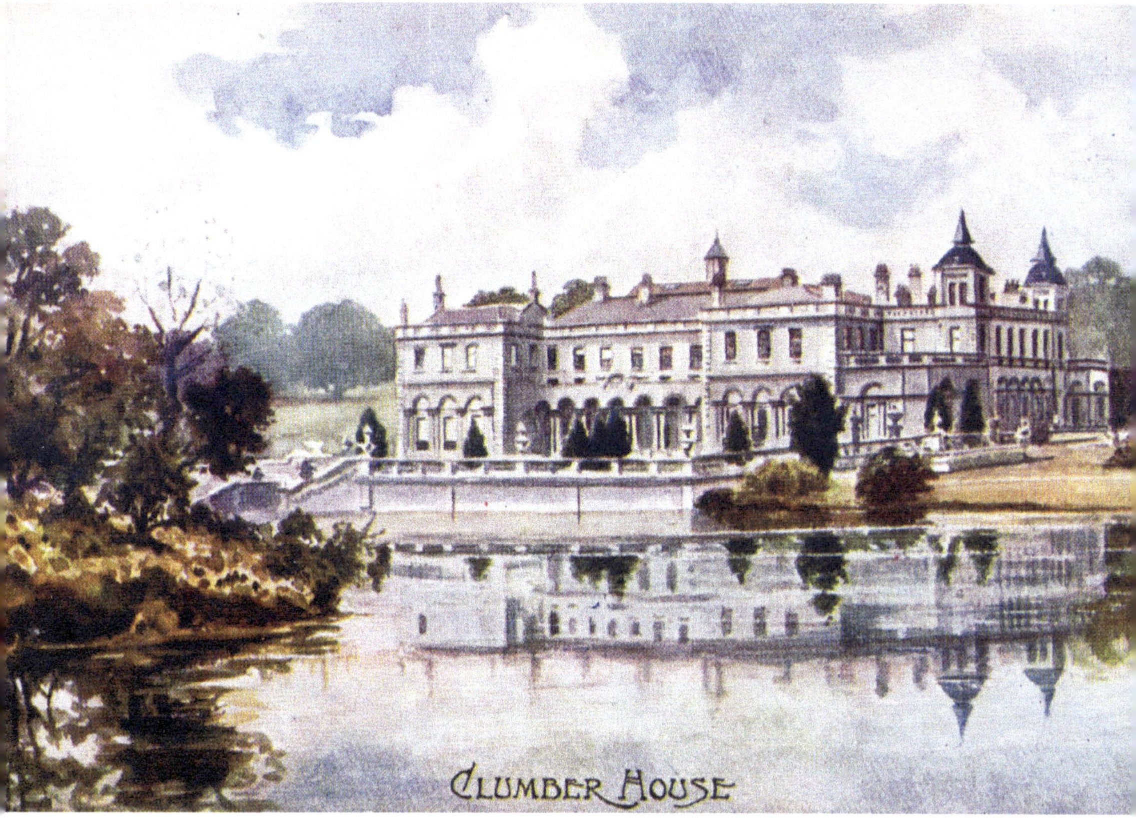

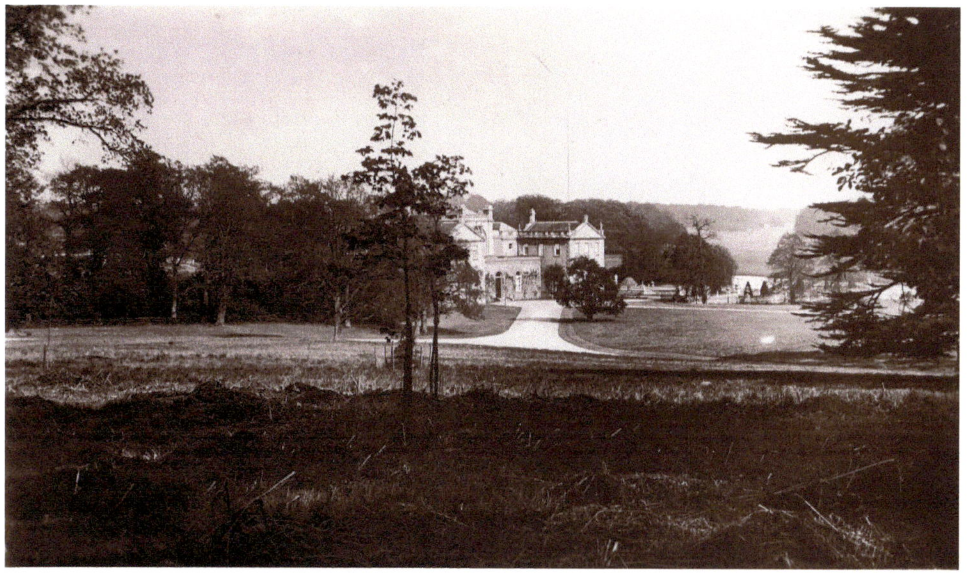

A classic view of Clumber House, early 1900s.

Clumber House from the rear, early 1900s.

Many houses, from modest country seats to grand estates, were demolished, and lands were scattered among smaller, individual farmers. Clumber House and its park survived to the 1930s, when the bulk of the house was demolished. It was intended that a smaller, replacement house would be built in the park following the dismantling, but this never happened. The main buildings on the site today include the church, the muniment room and duke's study, the walled kitchen garden (recently restored), the main gatehouses and estate buildings, plus other associated ornamental structures around the lake.

As Clumber House and its formal gardens and terraces were ripped apart, the materials and contents were sold piecemeal. The famous marble staircase, the stunning fountain, plus over half a mile of stone balustrading from the terraces all went under the hammer. The fountain alone was a huge marble structure cut from a solid block, and weighing over 50 tons. It had a lower basin of 12 feet 6 inches across and an upper one of 4 feet in diameter, supported by four marble dolphins. Its contents having been removed or sold off, the future of the estate and the park was in serious doubt. Like many such places it could well have gone for farming or even for development. However, following major public interest and concern, supported by public and local authority subscription, the estate ultimately passed to the National Trust in 1946. Clumber Park was bought for the future enjoyment of the public, and is now one of the main public Country Parks in the English Midlands and one of the most popular visitor destinations in the region.

Stand by the waterside terraces as the light is failing on a quiet weekday afternoon, and gaze across the lake. You can almost imagine the scene with the great house still intact, and the ship moored across on the far shoreline.

Welbeck Abbey

If Clumber is perhaps the best known of the remaining great houses of the Dukeries, then Welbeck is surely the least known, or certainly the least visible to the public. The entire estate, the house in particular, is shrouded by an aura of mystery and myth. Even today, the owners are notoriously suspicious of visitors. Add the history of eccentric aristocrats and remarkable architecture, and then there is a recipe for a unique piece of very English heritage. Indeed, because the estate and buildings survive largely intact, and the place is unaffected by tourists, Welbeck is one of the most authentic English country estates that exists. Little has changed since its Victorian heyday. Today the home of the Bentinck family, it is made abundantly clear that, with a few exceptions where footpaths exist, the public are not welcomed in the grounds. The buildings and landscape have been described as being on a gargantuan scale, and that is appropriate. This is indeed a spectacular house in an impressive and substantial estate.

Welbeck Abbey at the heart of this estate was founded as a religious house in 1140. With the Dissolution of the Monasteries, it passed into private hands. Over the centuries, successive generations of owners changed, extended and embellished the house and grounds. After the Second World War, the Portlands leased Welbeck to the Ministry of Defence for use as a sixth-form military training college. Grand, fully furnished state rooms were maintained, but the family no longer occupied the main building, instead choosing to occupy a smaller residence in the grounds, Welbeck Woodhouse. This lesser house was built in 1930–31 to a design by Walter Brierley. It is on the northern side of the estate and was built for the then Marquess of Titchfield. The Army occupied part of the abbey and many outbuildings from 1953 to 2005, when the lease was given up and the family once again privately occupied the main house.

While the estate and grounds are still strictly private, there is a growing and vibrant community of residential properties, a working mixed home farm, managed woodlands, artists' and makers' workshops, the Harley Gallery, the Welbeck Farm Shop, the Limehouse Café, Stitchelton Dairy, and the Welbeck Bakehouse. Furthermore, there are additional developments planned for a wide range of creative industries and arts in and around the estate.

By 1584, Welbeck was owned by Gilbert Talbot, who became 7th Earl of Shrewsbury, and was the son of the 6th Earl, of Mary, Queen of Scots, fame. As stepson of Bess of Hardwick, Bess arranged his marriage to her own daughter, Mary Cavendish, and thus linked two enormously rich and powerful strands. Further intrigue and manipulation by Bess resulted in Welbeck being owned by her third son Charles Cavendish and occupied by him and his wife Catherine. The latter was the daughter and heiress of Cuthbert Lord Ogle, and so both the barony of Ogle and the Welbeck Abbey Estate were inherited by Sir Charles and Catherine, and their son William. The latter was the famous William Cavendish, staunch Royalist, skilled equestrian and ambitious politician. He entertained both James I and Charles I at Welbeck and his other seat at Bolsover Castle, and gained titles such as Duke of Newcastle-upon-Tyne. His fortunes waned with the Royalists after the Civil War. The house became the principal family seat of the early dukes of Newcastle, who made significant additions to the house. The building work included the magnificent riding house commissioned by the 1st Duke and built by John Smithson. As the home of powerful and influential figures, monarchs were entertained here, and, at times, eminent authors and poets too. Welbeck passed down through the Cavendish family into the Portland line of descent, and ultimately became the main seat of the Dukes of Portland.

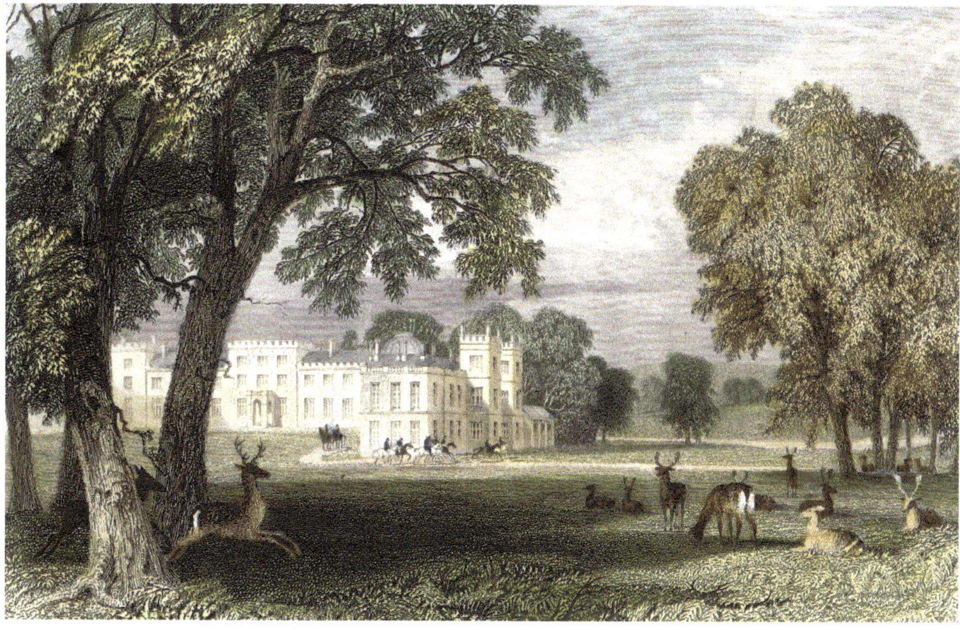

Welbeck Abbey and park with fallow deer.

Because of the war, William went abroad to Holland until the Restoration of the monarchy. Here he carried on his interests in breeding and training horses, and observed the growing ideas in Europe about estate management and land 'improvement'. When he returned to Welbeck he applied these new ideas to the great estates that he owned.

However, it is in the 5th Duke of Portland that we find one of the most enigmatic figures in this distinguished family tree. In 1800, Lord William John Cavendish-Scott-Bentinck was born as the younger son of the 4th Duke of Portland. On the sudden death of his older brother, Lord Titchfield, he became heir to the estate in 1821. While there was yet no sign of his coming eccentricities, which subsequently became famous to the point of legend, his love for the Covent Garden singer Adelaide Kemble was not returned. Subsequently, he never married, while in 1843 she married Edward John Sartoris, and retired after a brief but brilliant career. Whether this unhappy circumstance tipped the balance, who knows? For a while, William was MP for Kings Lynn, but rumours grew about his solitary habits and the way he shunned contact with his peers. As time passed the eccentricity grew, and while informed on world events, he was out of touch with the world immediately around him. Throughout the Victorian period he still wore clothes fashionable in Georgian times.

Seeking to avoid contact, the duke began to build, spending millions of pounds in constructing miles of underground passages and rooms, all lit by gaslight. When he travelled out, he went by carriage with the blinds drawn. He could travel underground in his carriage and then to a private train, again blinds drawn, if he travelled to London. Apparently, even the servants and men involved in the construction works were instructed to ignore him. Unprecedented for the time, they were told not to salute him, but to treat him 'as if he were a tree'. The now-famous underground ballroom is the largest room in Europe without supporting pillars.

Yet despite all of this, accounts by servants and others who knew him suggest that he was a kind and considerate man. Though taciturn, he was considered handsome, and certainly not afflicted, as was rumoured at the time, with some disfiguring skin disease. He was a passionate horseman and had a huge riding stable built, in size second only to the Spanish Riding School in Vienna. As the work continued in the buildings and on the estate, the duke essentially camped in four or five rooms in the house. Indeed, when the 6th Duke inherited, as there were no floors in some rooms, he had to pick his way carefully across them on supporting planks to get to the inner parts of the house. All the rooms were painted in pink, with parquet floors; all were bare and without furniture, except that virtually every room had a toilet in the corner. The 5th Duke died in December 1879, in his London home at Harcourt House. On his death there followed a lawsuit pursued by a man named Druce who claimed to be the legitimate son of the duke by his wife, a woman from a poor social background. It was claimed that William had secretly married this woman using the name Druce, and that she had run a bazaar in London's Baker Street. Though generally assumed bogus, the issue became the subject of widespread interest and gossip for many years.

While William hid away, his brother, Lord George Bentinck, was an able politician and an important figure in English horseracing circles during the nineteenth century. Known to Benjamin Disraeli as Lord Paramount of the Turf, George had persuaded his father, the 4th Duke, to loan Disraeli money to purchase the Hughenden Estate. This step meant that Disraeli was qualified as a 'landed Proprietor' and was thus able to lead the Protectionist Party in the

Commons, and so to aspire to the premiership. George himself was considered a possible future Prime Minister, but dropped dead while on a walk between Welbeck and the nearby Thoresby. He was only in his forties, and William, the 6th Duke of Portland, built a monument to his memory. This is inscribed as follows:

> To the memory of Lord George Bentinck, M.P. for Kings Lynn, third son of the fourth Duke of Portland who died suddenly near this spot on the 24th September, 1848 in his 48th year. This monument is raised by his kinsman William Arthur sixth Duke of Portland K.G., A.D. 1912.

On the succession to the 6th Duke, Welbeck was transformed yet again; from dark, secretive home of a recluse to a glittering centre of the English social scene. The duke and duchess entertained here for fifty years, with heads of state, kings, queens, and other distinguished people from around the world visiting. William Arthur was hugely successful, including in his horseracing activities. Much of his winnings from races such as the Derby twice were invested back into charitable projects such as almshouses and hospitals. Other members of the family, such as William's half-sister Ottolien Bentinck, moved in the circles of artists and writers of the time. Between 1914 and 1919, as with many great houses, parts were given over to the war effort. In this case, the kitchen block was used as an Army hospital.

Henry Bentinck, sixth cousin of Victor, succeeded to the earldom of Portland, and the title of earl passed down to Timothy Charles Robert Noel Bentinck, 12th Earl of Portland, 8th Count Bentinck und Waldeck Limpurg, in 1997. Born in June 1953, Tim Bentinck is an actor most widely known for his long-running role as David Archer in the BBC Radio 4 series *The Archers*. Although Tim Bentinck took his seat in the unreformed House of Lords, he did not speak there before the right to do so was lost with the House of Lords Act 1999. He generally does not use the titles.

In recent times, there has been a separation of the occupation of the estate and the titles. The descendants of the Cavendish Bentinck family still live at Welbeck. Up until her death on 29 December 2008, Lady Anne Cavendish-Bentinck, the elder daughter of the 7th Duke, lived at Welbeck Woodhouse, and owned most of the 17,000-acre estate. While she was unmarried, her younger sister, Lady Victoria Margaret Cavendish-Bentinck (1918–55), had married Gaetano Parente, Prince of Castel Viscardo. Their son William Henry Marcello Parente (born 1951) inherited the estates from his aunt Lady Anne. This inheritance included 15,000 acres on the Welbeck Abbey Estate and around 45,000 acres elsewhere in the East Midlands. Following the departure of the Ministry of Defence in 2005, the abbey has been home to William Parente, the only grandchild of the 7th Duke of Portland. Parente was High Sheriff of Nottinghamshire from 2003 to 2004.

The remarkable story of Welbeck continues, and while the estate remains strictly private, other initiatives are developing. So for example, in 2006, two directors from the School of Artisan Food began work on an 'artisan bakery' in the premises of the old fire station on the estate. With two large, wood-fired ovens, they felt this was a perfect location to teach aspiring artisan bakers.

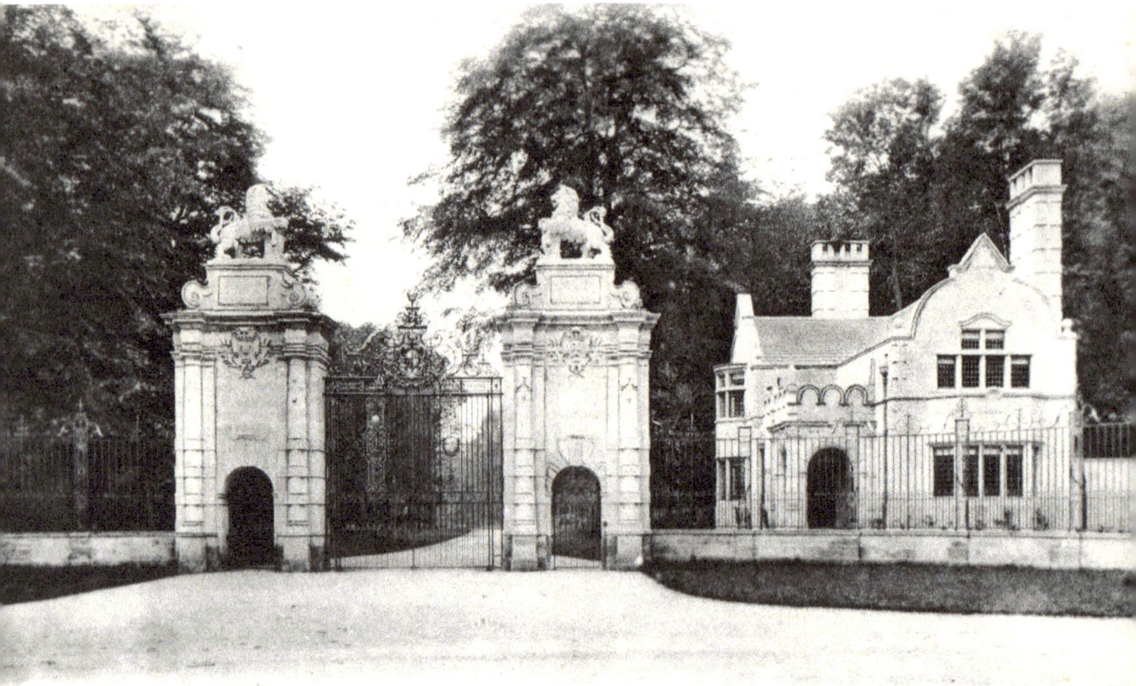

Above: A grand entrance to a grand estate – Welbeck Lodge and Gate, Worksop.

Below: The remarkable underground ballroom, Welbeck Abbey, 1920s.

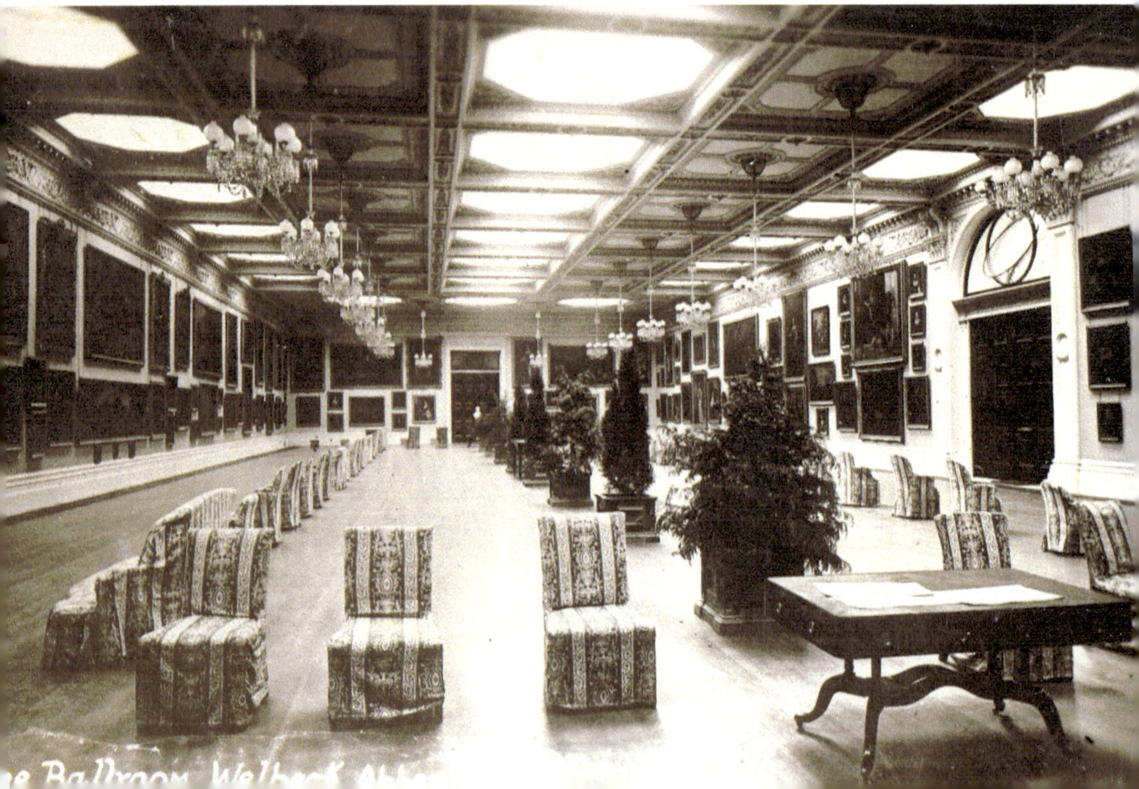

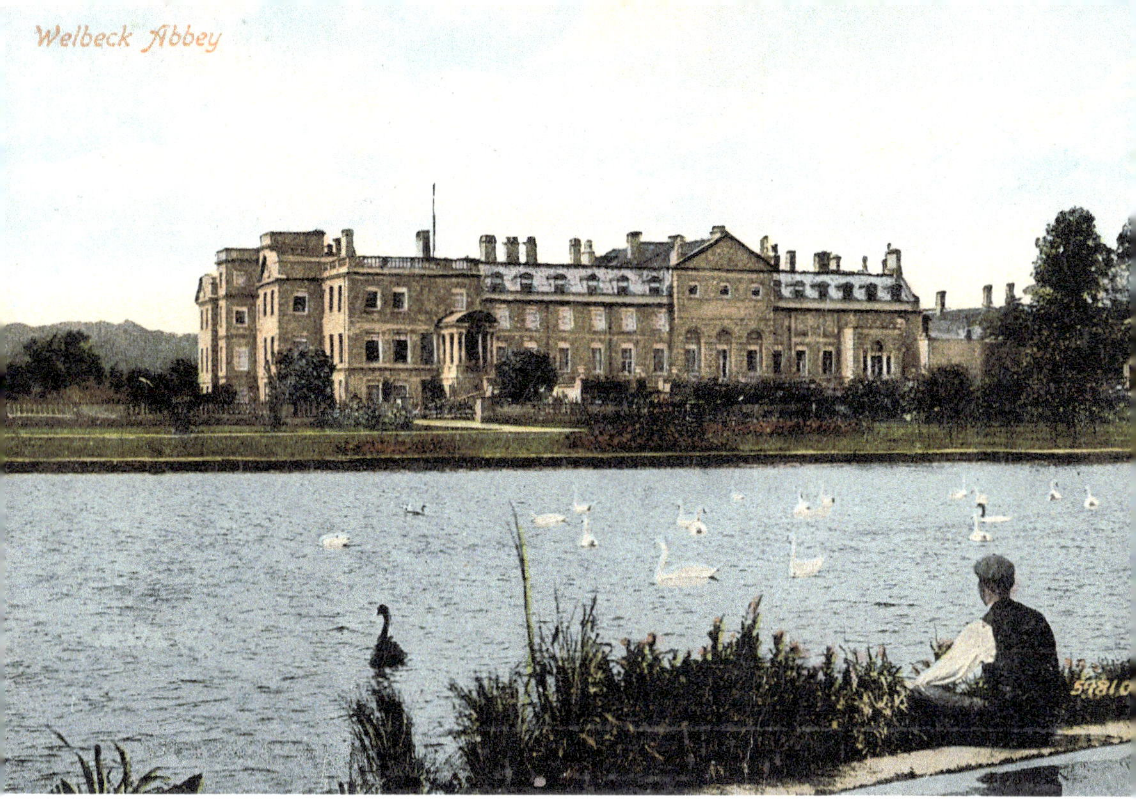

Above: Welbeck Abbey from the lake, 1918.

Below: Welbeck Abbey across the lake with punter in the foreground.

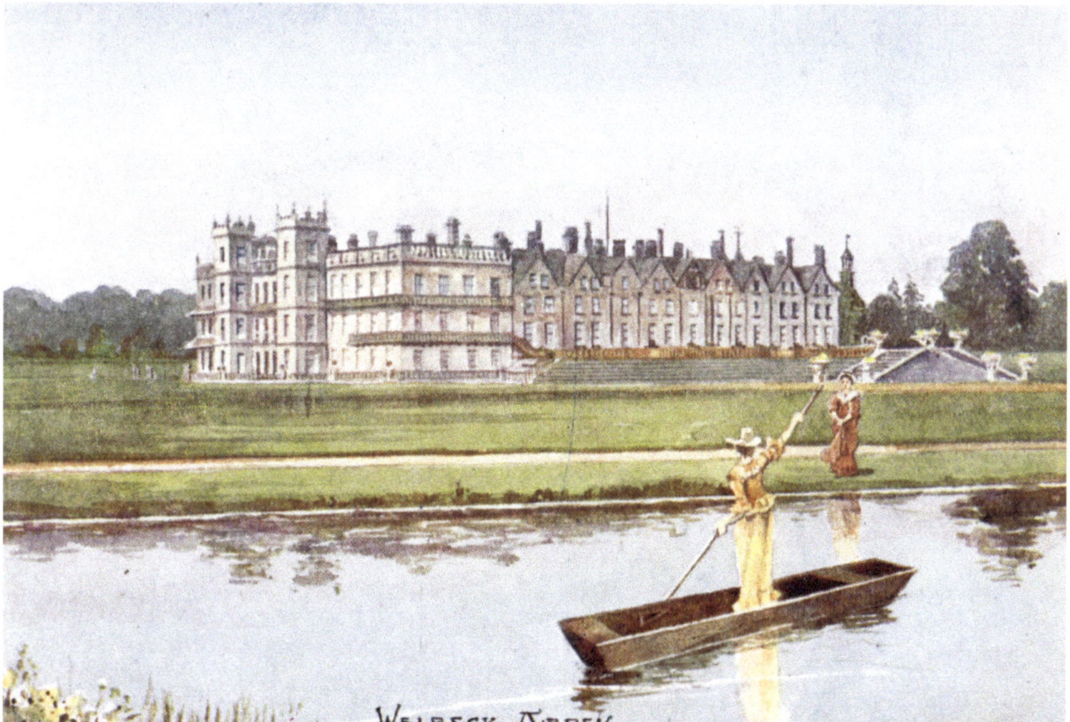

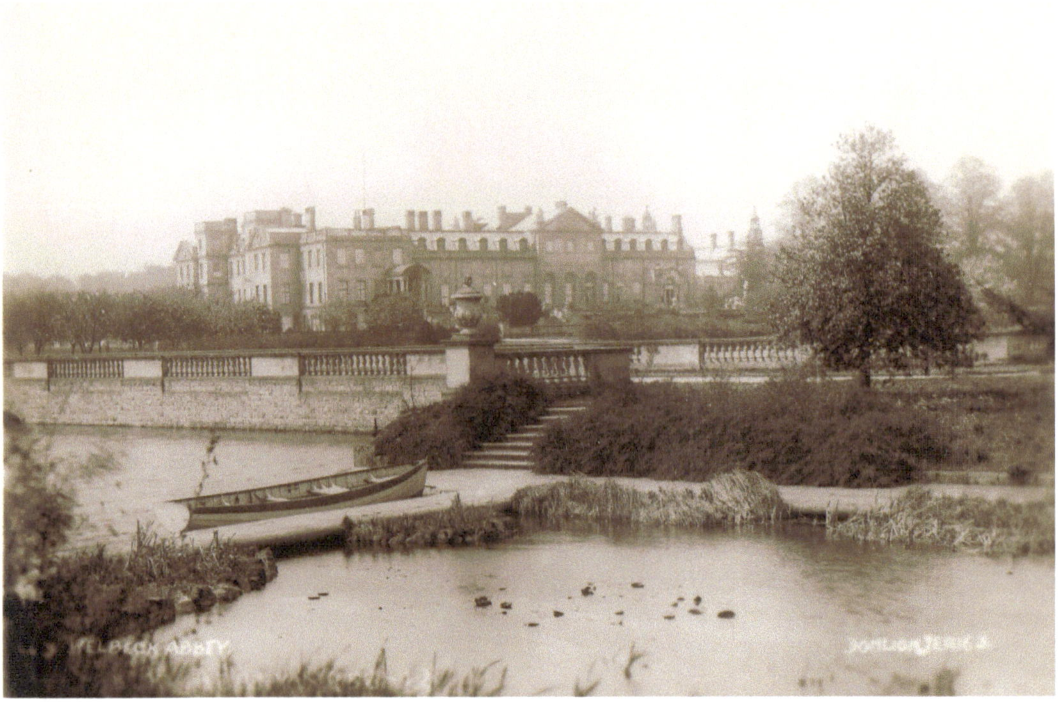

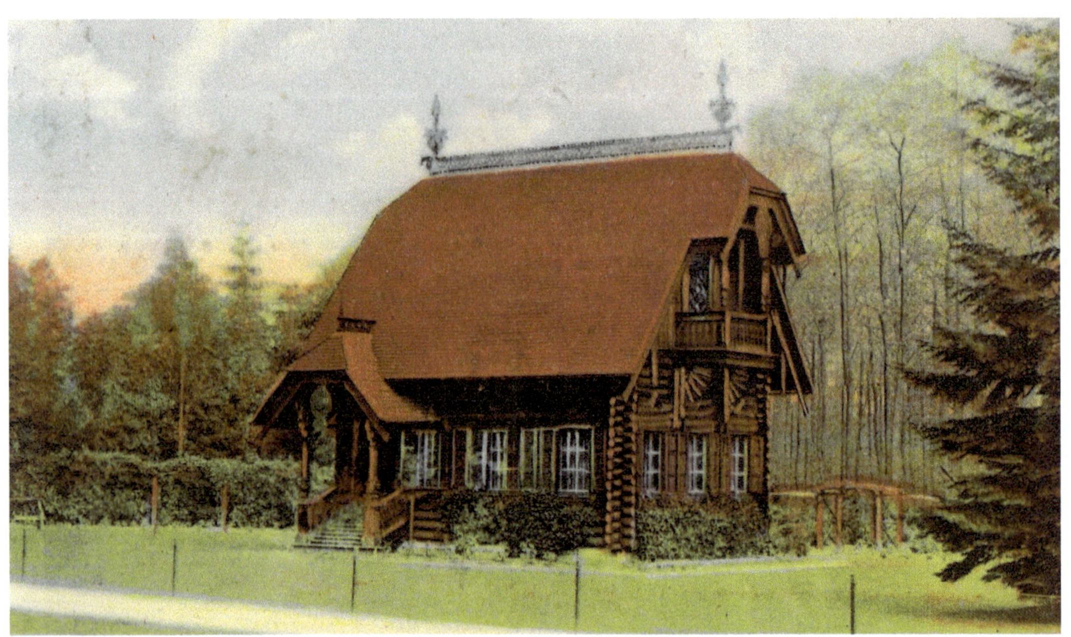

Welbeck Abbey, early 1900s.

The Russian shooting box, Welbeck.

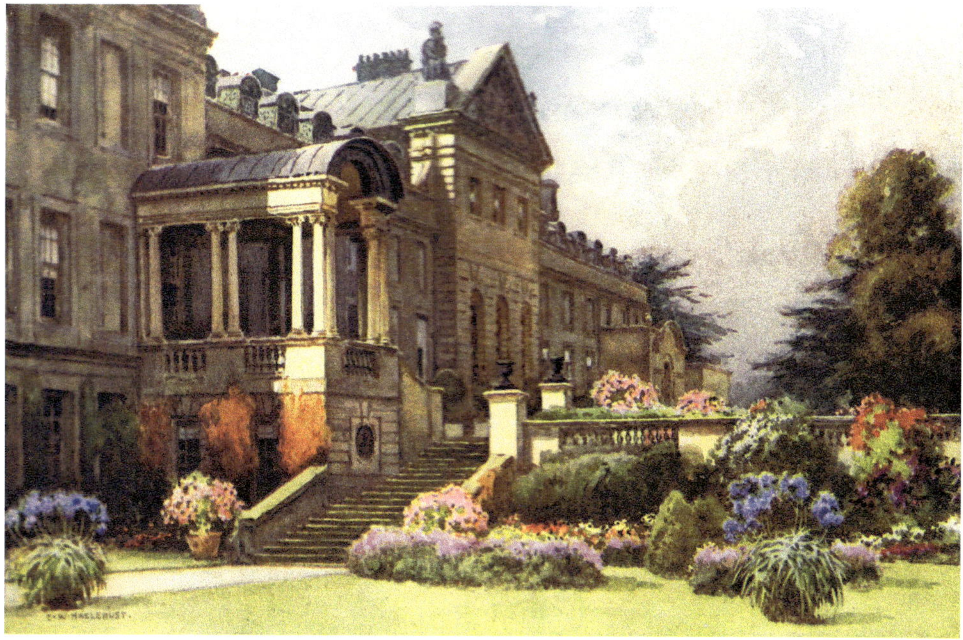

An intimate view of Welbeck Abbey garden.

Thoresby Hall

The fourth of our great Dukeries houses is Thoresby Hall, now a privately owned sumptuous hotel and spa. The present Thoresby Hall is a splendid monument to Victorian excess, and dates from around 1875, designed by Anthony Salvin, with gardens by Sir Humphrey Repton, and parkland by Capability Brown. The mansion was home to the Manvers family until the death of the 8th Earl in 1955. Today, if you stand in the remarkable great hall and gaze upwards, through the three storeys, to the open hammer-beam roof and minstrels' gallery, you experience a rich flavour of Thoresby's heraldic sense of place and purpose. The Pierrepont coat of arms dominates the huge stone fireplace. Robert de Pierrepont was said to have accompanied William I during the Norman Conquest of 1066, and was the ancestor of Thoresby's original owner Earl Manvers. In 1633, Richard Pierrepont, the 1st Earl of Kingston and another grandson of Bess of Hardwick, bought the house, which had occupied the site for about thirty-five years. In the 1680s, the 4th Earl of Kingston replaced that building, and then, in 1771, the 2nd Duke rebuilt the house in the Palladian style. In the 1950s, the seminal writer on English architecture, Sir Nicholas Pevsner, wrote of Thoresby: 'Here is a case where a mansion of the proudest is still completely inhabited and used as it was when the era of Disraeli conceived it.'

Thoresby sits in extensive parklands, woodlands and plantations extending to Ollerton in the south and to the Welbeck boundary in the north. The building is a monumental statement of social status and the security of a hierarchy of the time, which extended from the great nobility to the lowest servant or peasant. The great towers, windows and gables of Thoresby must have made the unrest and the threat of urban mobs or nouveau riche industrialists seem an era away. The 3rd Earl Manvers decided to move from a comfortable, old mansion by the lake to a purpose-built Elizabethan-style palace high on the hill above the surrounding lands. This is a bold statement of political and social authority and status and it was planned to 'stand for a thousand years'. Little could he foresee the dramatic changes that would sweep the landscape of the next century; it is remarkable that the house survives at all.

The name Pierrepont suggests Norman extraction, but the first fully reliable documentation is Sir Henry Pierrepont; the family tree is quite difficult to follow because of the numbers of Henrys and Roberts over several centuries. In the late thirteenth century, Henry de Pierrepont (d. 1292) married heiress Annora de Manvers of Holme, near Nottingham. Holme Pierrepont, situated south of the River Trent, became the main family seat for some centuries, and, now open to the public, it is still occupied by descendants of the family. Annora de Manvers (d. 1314), was the daughter of Michael de Manvers, and sister and heiress of Lionel de Manvers (d. *c.* 1284).

The medieval Pierreponts were prominent local landowners and politicians, two of whom were distinguished on the battlefield – Sir Robert de Pierrepont in the fourteenth century, and Sir Henry Pierrepont in the fifteenth century. Sir Henry's son Sir Robert de Pierrepont (d. 1334) fought against Sir Robert Bruce at Methven under Edward, Prince of Wales. He became Governor of Newark Castle in the reign of Edward II, and one of the chief English commanders in the army fighting against the Scots in 1327. He fought with the king in the Battle of Hallidown in 1333. Sir Henry Pierrepont (d. 1463) fought for the House of York in the Wars of the Roses.

Robert Pierrepont (1584–1643), was the Governor of Newark Castle, and became Lord Pierrepont, Viscount Newark and 1st Earl of Kingston-upon-Hull. With the advent of civil war, though after some delay, he naturally joined the Royalists and became Lieutenant-General of Lincoln, Rutland, Huntingdon, Cambridge and Norfolk. He had initially tried to remain neutral, declaring that 'when I take arms with the King against parliament, or with the parliament against the King, let a cannon-ball divide me between them'. He was the second son of Sir Henry Pierrepont (1546–1615) of Holme Pierrepont, Nottinghamshire, and Frances Cavendish. Frances was the daughter of the Rt Hon. Sir William Cavendish and Elizabeth Hardwick. Robert's sister was Grace, Lady Manners of Haddon Hall. In 1601, he married Gertude Talbot, daughter of Henry Talbot (1554–96). Henry was the son of George Talbot, the 6th Earl of Shrewsbury, and Elizabeth Reyner. While defending Gainsborough he was taken prisoner by Parliamentarians and accidentally killed on 25 July 1643 while being conveyed to Hull. His son Henry succeeded him. It was in 1633 that Sir Robert Pierrepont purchased the Thoresby Estate.

The 2nd Earl of Kingston, a staunch Royalist, accompanied Charles I to Oxford. Further to the titles he inherited from his late father, he was created Marquess of Dorchester. Henry was someone eccentric, renowned as both a scholar and a man of violent temper, much prone to duels. He studied law and was called to the Bar, and also studied medicine, leaving a fine medical library to the Royal College of Physicians. When he died a bachelor in 1680, the marquessate became extinct, though the earldom continued and was inherited in turn by each of three great-nephews. The third of these was Evelyn Pierrepont, the 5th Earl of Kingston, a man who was both handsome and clever, and a firm Hanoverian. In due course, he was rewarded by Queen Anne with the re-establishment of the Marquessate of Dorchester. Then, with the accession to the throne of George I, he became Duke of Kingston and a privy councillor.

His daughter was Lady Mary Pierrepont, a feisty individual who made her mark in both literature and medicine. After eloping with Edward Wortley-Montagu, a diplomat, she spent time in the exotic environs of Turkey, where she observed local natives using primitive inoculation. She applied this to her own son, probably saving him from smallpox. Along with the doctor, Edward Jenner, Mary fought against suspicion and ignorance to introduce smallpox inoculation to Great Britain. Her brother died before inheriting the estates and the titles, and so the dukedom passed to Evelyn Pierrepont, the 2nd Duke of Kingston. The new duke went through a marriage ceremony with Elizabeth Chudleigh, though as it turned out, she had been secretly married to the Hon. Augustus Hervey, a Naval lieutenant, poor and down on his luck. However, after a somewhat disastrous marriage, and Hervey's realisation that he was to inherit the Earldom of Bristol, he had decided it was time to be rid of Elizabeth. She already had a reputation for scandalous behaviour and so he sued for divorce, at which point she denied that the marriage had ever taken place. A court ruling followed, which stated that technically she was a spinster. By this time, she was already the mistress of the Duke of Kingston and he 'married' her. When the duke died, he had left her all his property for life, though the dukedom became extinct. However, there was a final heir to the family fortune, in the shape of Evelyn's nephew Charles Meadows. Now heir to the estate, Meadows began proceedings against the 'duchess' for bigamy. By this time, Elizabeth was also legally Countess of Bristol, and as such, the House of Lords tried her. Remarkably, considering the earlier judgement, she was now found guilty, and Meadows succeeded to the Kingston estates, adopting the Pierrepont name and coat of arms. In 1796, he became Baron Pierrepont and Viscount Newark. The Kingston earldom was not possible now since in the Ireland peerage, the King family had already been made earls of Kingston. Bearing this in mind, Charles Meadows went back to the early family history and the Pierrepont's first family residence with Annora de Manvers. The new title bestowed upon him was Earl Manvers, created in 1807.

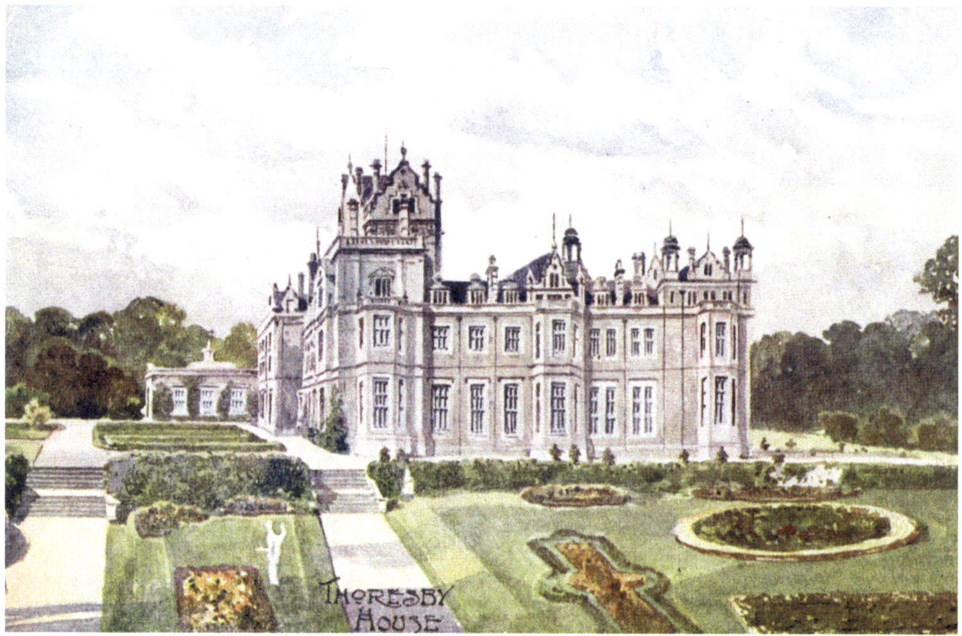

Thoresby House and formal gardens, early 1900s.

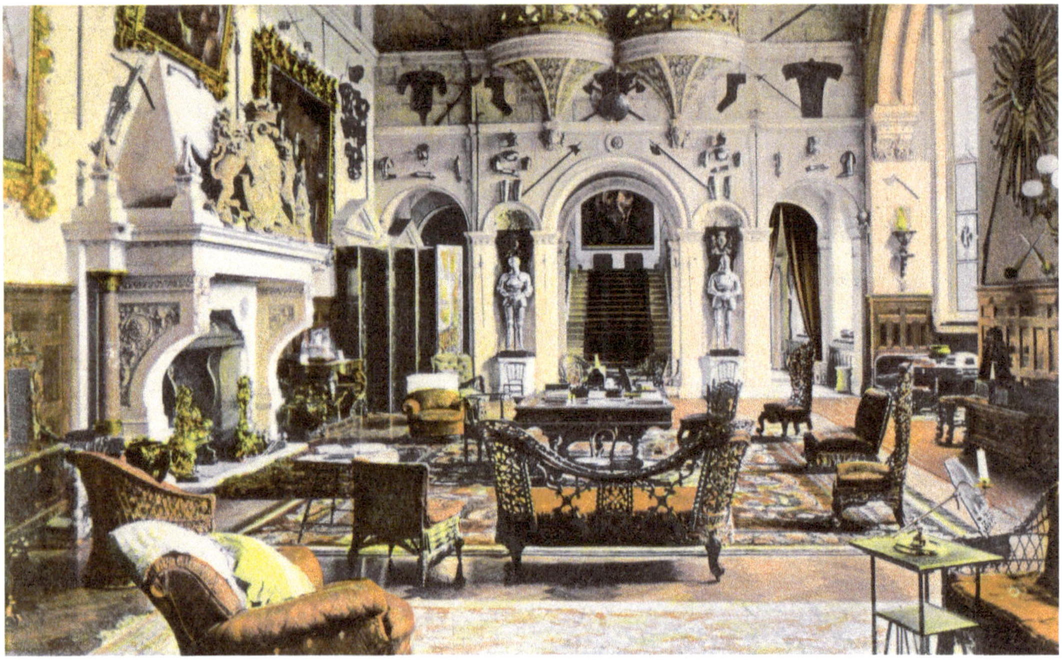

The lavishly spectacular Large Hall, Thoresby.

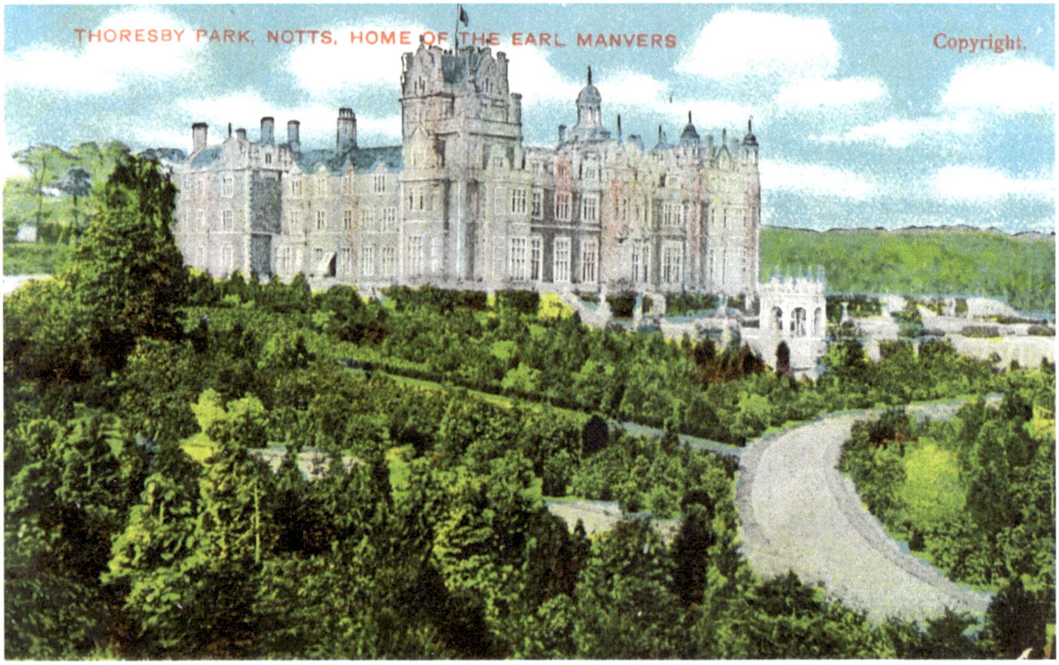

Thoresby Park, early 1900s, to show the spectacular location of the new house.

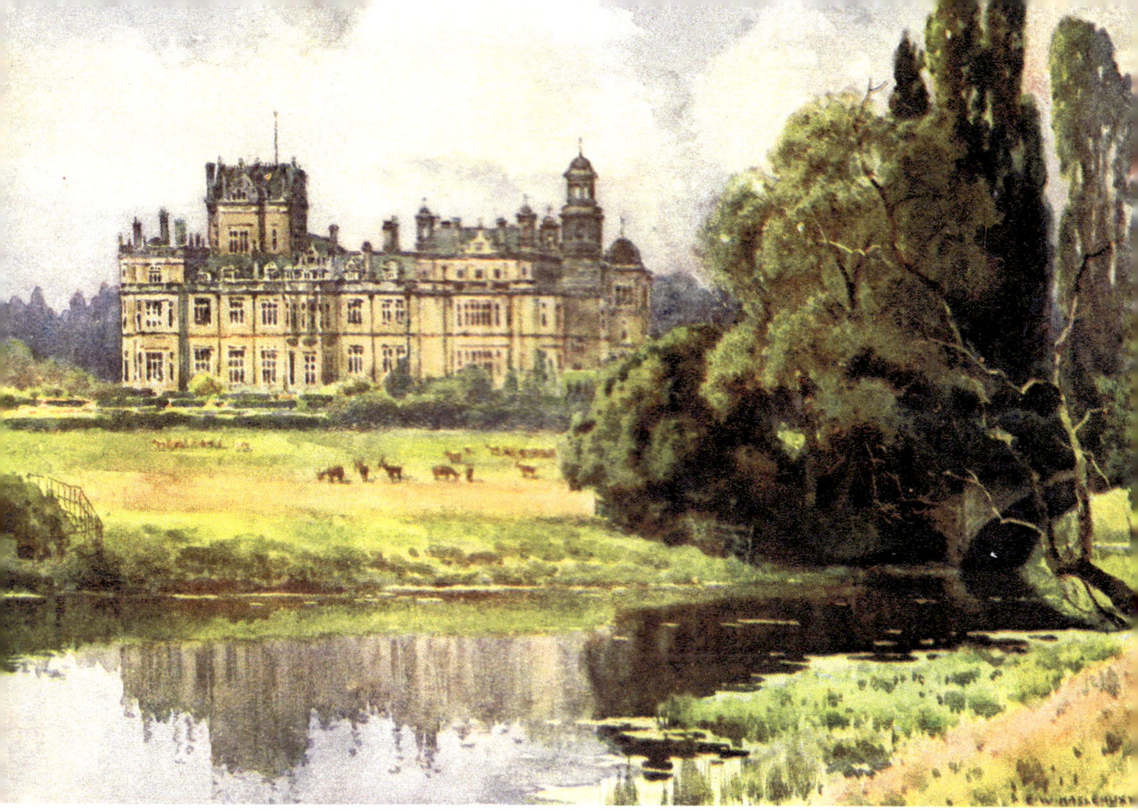

Above: Thoresby Hall.

Below: Thoresby House in its beautiful pastoral setting, 1905.

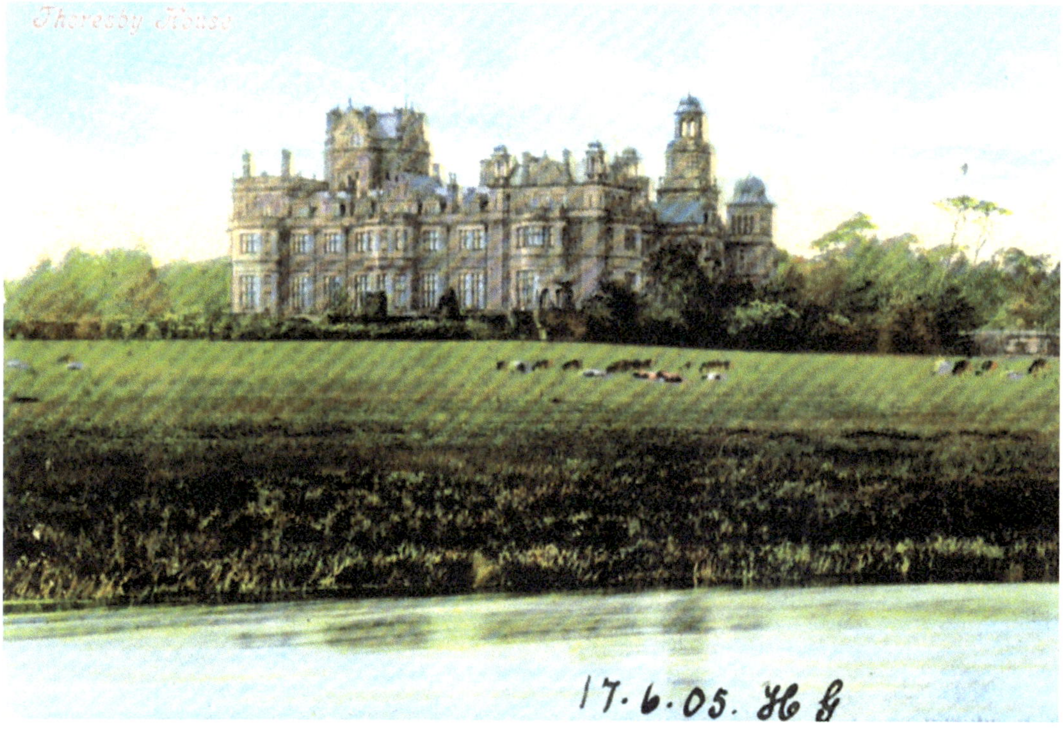

Rufford Abbey

The final great house is Rufford Abbey, now a mix of buildings, ruined shells, and extensive gardens. This great house, now sadly much reduced, was for a time one of the most impressive and dramatic residences in England. Today, the site is a country park, in 150 acres of historic parkland, woodland and gardens with ruins of a medieval monastery, a contemporary craft centre, gardens, woodland walks, a children's play village, a sculpture trail, a mill, and a lake. English Heritage manages the monastic ruins, described as the best-preserved remains of a Cistercian abbey west cloister range in England. They date mainly from around 1170, and are incorporated into part of a seventeenth-century and later mansion. The main building which once had elements of almost all major English architectural styles through the centuries, is now a shell.

In 1146, Gilbert de Gaunt, Earl of Lincoln, founded the Cistercian Abbey of St Mary the Virgin. The monks of this order were known as the 'white monks' because their habits were made of undyed wool. They valued an austere life based upon prayer and hard work. Rufford Abbey was moderately wealthy and supported a community of monks from its completion in about 1170 to its dissolution in 1536. In fact, Rufford was one of the first English abbeys affected by Henry VIII's suppression of the monasteries; the entire estate was quickly acquired by George Talbot, 4th Earl of Shrewsbury. The 6th Earl of Shrewsbury, from 1560 to 1590, converted the monastic buildings into a house. The earl was the fourth and final husband of Bess of Hardwick, by this time bitterly estranged from his domineering wife. In 1610, a further projecting wing was added to the northern end of the building. By 1626, Lady Mary Talbot, the sister of the seventh and eighth earls of Shrewsbury, inherited the estate. It passed ultimately to her husband, Sir George Savile (1551–1622), a Yorkshire baronet, and a long-term connection to that family began. This was one of the only major Sherwood estates outside Bess of Hardwick's direct control. Another point of distinction is that Rufford was technically not one of the 'Dukeries', since the incumbents never rose to those heights.

The inheritance of estates and tiles associated with Rufford down the centuries was incredibly complex, with many 'dead ends'. The 8th Earl never married but had several illegitimate children, four sons and one daughter, by a French woman. He died in a hunting accident in 1856 and bequeathed Rufford to his second natural son Captain Henry Lumley (d. 1881). On his death, they passed to the fourth son, Augustus William Lumley (1829–87). With the death of Augustus, the estates passed to Lord Scarborough's eldest natural son, Sir John Lumley-Savile, and he took the surname Savile. Created Baron Savile in 1888, he was a prominent diplomat, and the peerage was created with remainder to Savile's nephew John Lumley, who succeeded as second baron. In 1898 the latter assumed the surname of Savile in addition to that of Lumley. The title continues to the present day with his grandson, the 4th Baron, who succeeded his uncle in 2008. The second Lord Savile, now Lumley-Savile, was a friend of Prince Edward, later King Edward VII. Indeed, Edward would reside at Rufford when up for the Doncaster races or for the shooting, continuing long-standing royal tradition since James I and Charles II both visited.

However, the situation for Rufford took a downward turn in the 1930s. In 1938, the 3rd Baron Savile inherited the Rufford Estate as a minor, and his trustees split it into lots and sold it. The estate and house that had survived in the same family for around 400 years were broken up, and the contents was sold. The family estate, with gardeners, servants, cooks, stable-hands, and farm and forestry workers, was swept away as if it had never been. Just as with Clumber at about the same time, there was an enormous sale of goods and property. Sir Albert Ball, a Nottinghamshire industrialist, purchased the estates. His executors then sold on to Mr Henry Talbot de Vere Clifton, who intended to demolish the buildings. However, the county council stepped in to prevent this act of vandalism, but what followed was a gradual destruction of most of the above-ground structures.

In 1952, Nottinghamshire County Council bought the abbey and park, the north and east wings were demolished in 1956. The remaining west range and south service wing were placed in the care of the then Ministry of Works, and subsequently the Department of the Environment. Today, you approach the abbey from the car park and over a nineteenth-century Jacobean-style bridge. The roofed porch formed the original main entrance to the Earl of Shrewsbury's sixteenth-century house. Inner double doors lead into the now ruined Brick Hall, which was the grand reception room for the post-abbey residence and before that, the dormitory of the lay brothers. There is a fine late fourteenth-century window surrounded by carved heads and foliage. Today, in front of the night stair, is a large area of open lawn, the location of the original abbey church and the late seventeenth-century northern wing. An entrance leads to the original cellar and the monks' refectory, a nicely preserved example of Cistercian architecture. The room is plain, with the vaults supported by simple rounded and octagonal columns. There are still traces of the day stair and the alcoves that held linen and spoons for use in the refectory. Even now, the building gives a real feel for aspects of monastic life.

The fate of Rufford casts into a sharp light the good fortune of the great English houses that have survived. Given a little more fortune and foresight, Rufford too might have been saved intact. What happened here occurred at many other sites across the country, but few represent such tragic loss as evidenced by the remaining semi-ruin. This said, the country park and the remaining buildings are very pleasant, and in recent years the county council and English Heritage have done much to interpret and to enhance the site. Nevertheless, the loss through 'controlled demolition' over the decades has been both expensive and very sad. Much of the domestic residence was Elizabethan, but there were fine Georgian rooms with wonderful plasterwork. The destruction of the huge Stuart north wing, with its long gallery of more than 120 feet, was particularly tragic.

Like the other Dukeries houses and estates, Rufford has suffered because of deep coal mining and associated land subsidence. For a while, the lake was empty of water because of these impacts. It is now restored, and the nearby sawmill has been converted to a shop and information centre. The lake has both ornamental and wild water birds, and the park has ornamental beds and ponds too. The ruins of the abbey and the secular house form a romantic backdrop to this popular park.

The site has important historic connections. As with the other great houses, the figure of Bess of Hardwick looms large. In particular, Bess had ambitious plans for her offspring. Herself a powerful woman, she probably harboured ideas of her children achieving even more. Bess managed to arrange a marriage between her daughter Elizabeth and the Earl of Lennox. The earl was the brother of Lord Darnley, and so close to the succession to the throne. The marriage ceremony took place in the private chapel at Rufford, but the scheming ended tragically as the earl, only aged twenty-one years, died two years later. The one child from the union was Lady Arabella Stuart (1575–1615), an unfortunate pawn in the political games of the time. Arabella was considered a threat by both Elizabeth I and then by James I, and spent the last days of her short life in the Tower of London, where she died. In her final days, Lady Beauchamp (her married name) refused food and consequently fell ill. She died on 25 September 1615, and was buried in Westminster Abbey on 29 September of that year. In the nineteenth century, during a search for the tomb of James I, Arabella's lead coffin was located in a royal vault, placed directly on top of that of Mary, Queen of Scots.

Apparently, the ghost of Lady Arabella stalked the corridors of Rufford Abbey, and indeed, this was one of the most haunted houses in England. Apparitions included a cold, clammy baby that would get into bed with you at night, most disconcerting! One story of this ghost was by Vita Sackville-West, the English author, poet and gardener, with a famously lascivious lifestyle, an open bisexual marriage and more. Her mother, Lady Sackville, had taken her to Rufford and the child slept in a small bed in the same room as her. During the night, a small child that crept into the bed and nestled beside her woke Lady Sackville; assuming it was her daughter Vita, she thought no more about it. In the morning however, it was clear that the daughter had never strayed from her own bed.

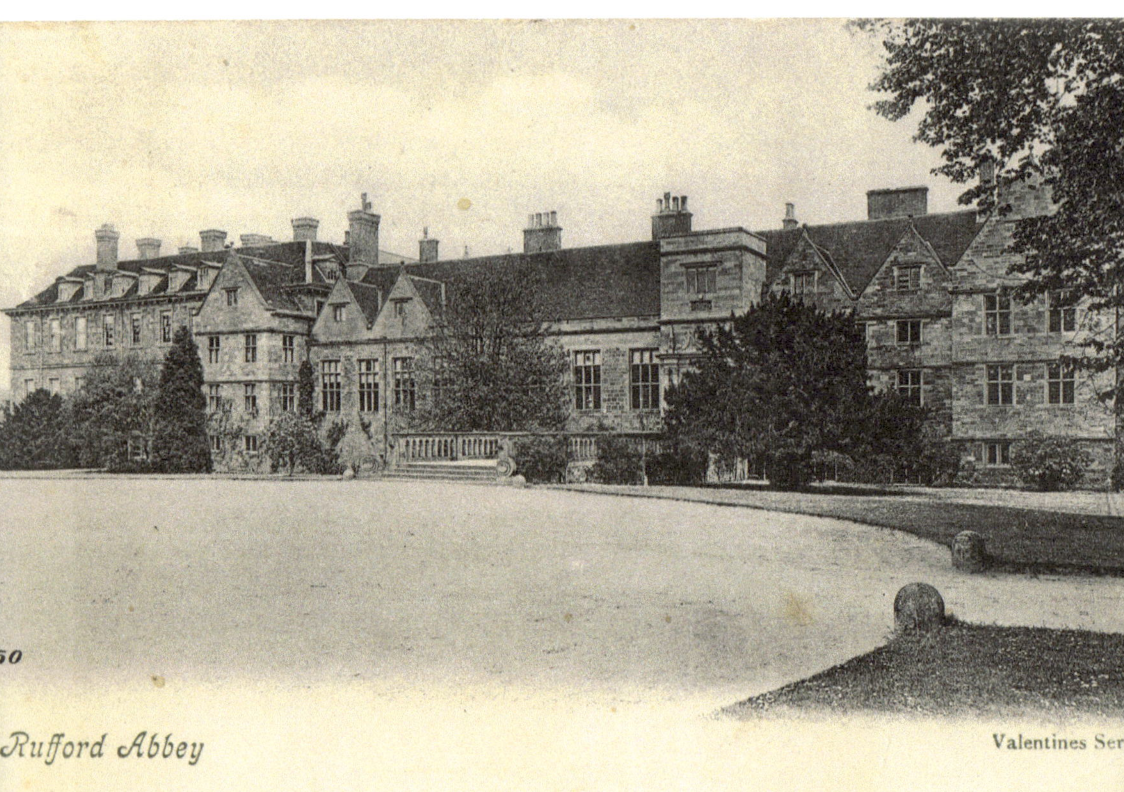

The once great Rufford Abbey, 1907.

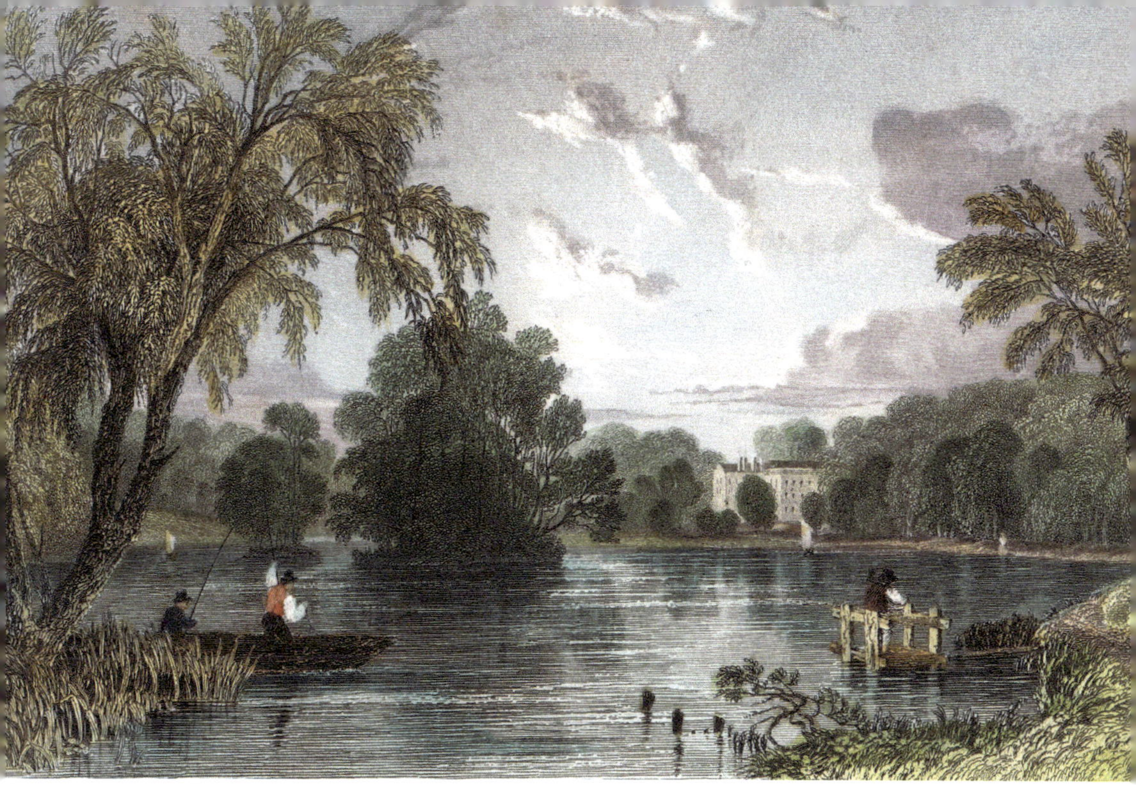

Rufford Abbey from the lake, early 1800s.

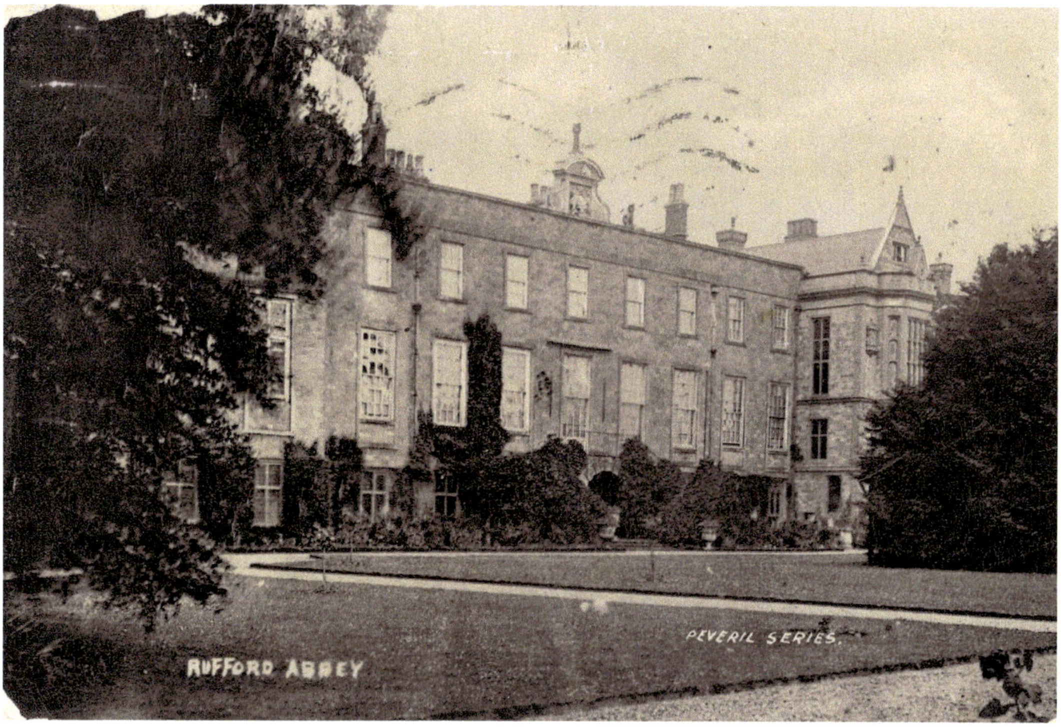

Rufford Abbey, 1915.

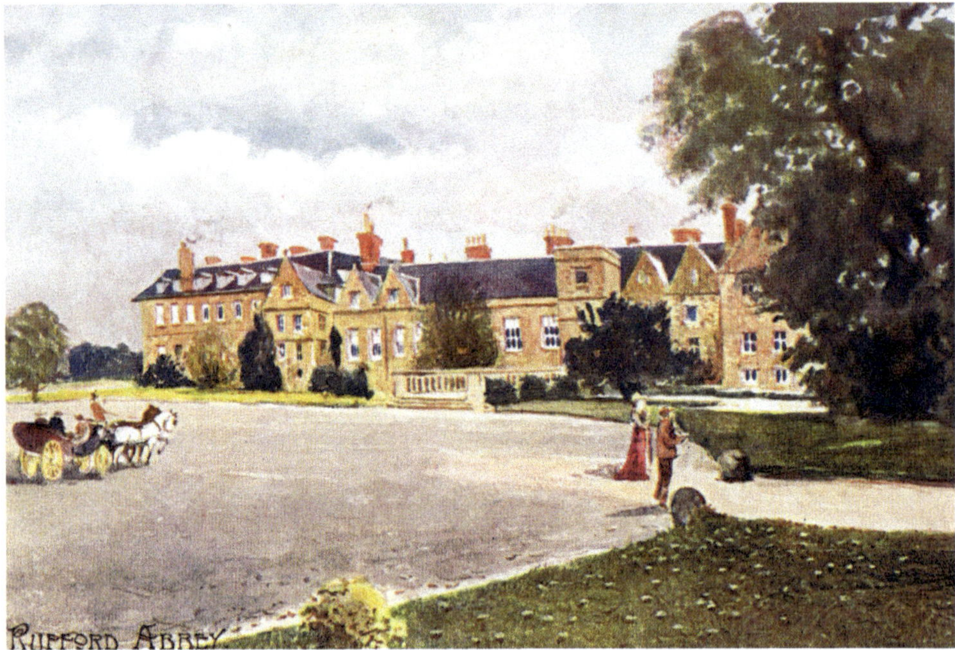

Rufford Abbey, early 1900s.

Bolsover Castle

At the western edge of the Sherwood region, the small town of Bolsover has suffered catastrophic impacts of coal mining and associated chemical works, followed by post-industrial decline and high unemployment. However, it does boast one of the jewels of the English Midlands, Bolsover Castle. This stunning baroque building stands on a spectacular west-facing location now overlooking the M1 motorway. Like Welbeck, in 1608, Sir Charles Cavendish purchased Bolsover manor and castle from Gilbert, Earl of Shrewsbury. Sir Charles then began the process of rebuilding the castle, continued by his son, William, 1st Duke of Newcastle-upon-Tyne. William was responsible for building the large indoor riding school at Bolsover and for providing lavish entertainment there for King Charles I.

The seat passed down through the Portland line and in 1945, the 7th Duke of Portland gave the property to the nation. Today, Bolsover Castle is owned and managed by English Heritage and has had extensive restoration, including the riding school.

The town still boasts some nice buildings and the spectacular Bolsover Castle, described in glowing terms by Sacheverell Sitwell who stated that 'its romantic fire must touch and heat the blood of all who see it'.

Hodsock Priory

Like many great halls and houses of the Dukeries, Hodsock has a remarkable history, and much is not what it at first seems. This country house is about 4 miles north of Worksop, and 1 mile south of the small town of Blyth. In spite of its name, it is not and never has been a priory. Today it is known for its splendid displays of spring snowdrops. While the house is not open to visitors, the gardens and woods are open to the public during the February snowdrop season.

The Cressey family owned Hodsock for more than 200 years from the mid-twelfth century. An important family, they entertained kings at Hodsock, notably Henry II, John and Edward I. Then in the early thirteenth century, as leprosy spread northwards from the Mediterranean, they founded a leper hospital in nearby Blyth. Part of the building is still visible. In the early fifteenth century, the estate passed to the Clifton family, who subsequently owned it through fourteen generations until 1765. Though it was not their primary residence, they entertained Henry VIII there in 1541, but they spent little on its upkeep. On the side of the Royalists in the English Civil War in the 1640s, the family was fined heavily by Parliament and the house was reduced to little more than a farmstead.

In 1765, for the only time in its history, Hodsock was sold, by Sir Gervase Clifton, 6th Baronet, to the Mellish family, owners of an estate at Blyth. The combined estates were around 20,000 acres. William Mellish (d. 1771) and his son, Charles, were significant Nottinghamshire figures of their time. From Charles, Hodsock passed to a younger son, Colonel Henry Francis Mellish; the eldest son, Joseph, was disinherited because of his decadent and extravagant lifestyle. However, this was of little benefit, since Henry was also a lover of horseracing. Despite his horses twice winning the St Ledger in the early 1800s, he ran up gambling debts and lost the Blyth estate.

During the nineteenth century, with a now reduced estate, the house was twice rebuilt, and renamed Hodsock Priory. The first rebuilding was by Henry's sister, Anne Chambers, who inherited Hodsock when he lost his money. Architect Ambrose Poynter designed the south wing in the Gothic Revival style of the time. When Anne Chambers died, Hodsock passed to William Leigh Mellish and in 1873, his widow employed architect George Devey to alter and enlarge the house. Interestingly, Devey's style was to design country houses as if they had existed for centuries.

The now famous gardens at Hodsock were developed in the early twentieth century by head gardener Arthur Ford, a nationally known writer on gardening. However, because of his reputation, he was headhunted by Kew Gardens. As with many such gardens, during the Second World War, the Women's Land Army was accommodated in the house and turned the flowerbeds to vegetables. After 1945, the house stayed with the Mellish family, but land, furniture, books and paintings were sold. In 1966, the estate passed to Sir Andrew Buchanan, 5th Baronet, who relocated to the property and in 1991, became Lord Lieutenant of Nottinghamshire.

Newstead Abbey

Sold by Charles Fraser to philanthropist Sir Julien Cahn, Newstead Abbey and a museum of Byron memorabilia are today owned by Nottingham City Council. Cahn presented the house to Nottingham Corporation in 1931. Located between Nottingham and Mansfield, the house and the estate have a long, often tortuous and frequently romantic history, as found with many Sherwood locales. The link to the poet Lord Byron makes Newstead a place of global literary significance. The site is an ancient one, the priory of St Mary of Newstead, a house of Augustinian canons, founded about 1163. It was founded by King Henry II as one of many penances for the murder of Archbishop Thomas Becket. In 1534, the *Valor Ecclesiasticus*, a visitation of the monasteries of England commissioned by the king, gave an annual value of £167 16*s* 11½*d*. This report was the basis of the evaluation of the church's assets by Henry VIII, and the amount equates to about £70,000 today. At this time, it was recorded that in commemoration of Henry II as founder, 20 shillings were given to the poor on Maundy Thursday. Additionally, each day of the year, and at a value of 60 shillings, a portion of food and drink fit for a canon was given to a poor person. Newstead would clearly fall into the lesser category described by Henry's agents as the sort of place where 'manifest sin, vicious, carnal and abominable living is daily used and committed'. However, despite the annual value of Newstead being below the £200 threshold for the suppression of the lesser monasteries, the priory was exempted, on payment to the Crown, in 1537, of a considerable fine of £233 6*s* 8*d*.

Eventually, on 21 July 1539, the priory was surrendered, with documents signed by attached John Blake, prior, Richard Kychun, sub-prior, John Bredon, cellarer, and nine other canons, Robert Sisson, John Derfelde, William Dotton, William Bathley, Christopher Motheram, Geoffrey Acryth, Richard Hardwyke, Henry Tingker, and Leonard Alynson. Again, rather surprisingly, those in holy orders did pretty well out of the deal. The prior received a pension of £26 13*s* 4*d*, or about £10,000 today, the sub-prior £6, and the rest of the ten canons from £5 6*s* 8*d* to £3 6*s* 8*d*. However, with the Dissolution there also began a long period of destruction and pillaging of items deemed to be valuable and perhaps tainted by popery. When Newstead Abbey Lake was dredged in the late eighteenth century, the abbey's lectern was found where the monks had thrown it, in the fishponds. In 1805, the lectern was donated to Southwell Minster where it can still be seen.

On 26 May 1540, Henry VIII granted Newstead Abbey to Sir John Byron of Colwick and he began its conversion into a grand country house. Succeeded by his son Sir John Byron of Clayton Hall, numerous additions were made to the original buildings. As often the case, the thirteenth-century ecclesiastical buildings had been badly damaged during the Dissolution, and much new building with the old dressed stone was needed. The property then passed to John Byron MP, a Royalist commander in the English Civil War who distinguished himself at the First Battle of Newbury. He was made Baron Byron in 1643 because of his service to the Crown and his prowess in battle.

From John Byron, the estate moved to his brother Richard Byron, and to his son William, a minor poet. He in turn was succeeded in 1695 by his son William Byron, 4th Baron Byron. It was the fourth baron who, in the eighteenth century, began the substantial landscaping of the estate's gardens. William, 5th Baron Byron, added Gothic follies as Newstead evolved into a stately and romantic estate. However, eccentric and violent, it was the 5th Baron who gained the nickname 'the Wicked Lord', and was responsible for ruining Newstead. The trigger was when Lord Byron's son and heir (also named William), eloped with his cousin Juliana Byron, the daughter of William's brother, John Byron. The 5th Baron was passionately against the match since he claimed the inbreeding would lead to children plagued with madness. On a more pragmatic note, he was desperate for his heir to marry well in order to get the estate out of debt. Consequent on the defiance of the young lovers, he set about destroying the potential inheritance. In the event of his death, his son William would inherit only debt and worthless property. His actions plunged the house of Newstead into disrepair, with great stands of timber felled in the grounds and over 2,000 deer on the estate slaughtered. Ironically, his plans were thwarted by tragedy when in 1776, his son and heir died prematurely. The 5th Baron William even outlived his grandson, who, fighting in Corsica, was killed by cannon fire in 1794, aged twenty-two years. The 'Wicked Lord' lived to the ripe old age of seventy-nine years and died on 21 May 1798. Reputedly, at his death, great numbers of crickets that he apparently kept at Newstead Abbey left in swarms.

Therefore, by the nineteenth century, the title, house and estate of Newstead Abbey passed to the 5th Baron's great-nephew, George Gordon, the soon-to-be famous poet, who became the 6th Baron Byron. The famous Lord Byron was christened after his maternal grandfather, a descendant of King James I. Arriving at Newstead, the young Lord Byron was greatly impressed by the estate, which appealed to his extravagant taste and sense of his own importance. Nevertheless, the inheritance came with serious troubles, with an annual income of only £800, and investment was needed for urgent repairs. Consequently, Byron and his mother moved to Nottingham and neither resided permanently at Newstead. Yet his vision of the romantic ruin of the decayed Newstead was a metaphor for his own family's fall:

> Thro' thy battlements, Newstead, the hollow winds whistle;
> Thou, the hall of my fathers, art gone to decay.

From January 1803, the Newstead Estate was leased at £50 a year to Henry Edward Yelverton, the twenty-three-year-old 19th Baron Grey de Ruthyn. This was for five years, until Byron came of age. Although in 1803 Byron lived for a while with Lord Grey, they fell out badly. In 1808, at the end of the lease, Lord Grey left and Byron returned to live at Newstead, undertaking extensive and expensive repairs. However, much of the work was cosmetic rather than structural and most of the efforts decayed within a short time. Byron was famously fond of his Newfoundland dog called Boatswain, the inspiration for one of his most famous poems. Sadly, in 1808, the dog died of rabies and was buried at Newstead Abbey. His monument is larger than that of his master. The poem 'Epitaph to a Dog', as inscribed on Boatswain's monument, is one of Byron's best-known works:

> Near this Spot
> Are deposited the Remains
> of one
> Who possessed Beauty
> Without Vanity,
> Strength without Insolence,
> Courage without Ferosity,
> And all the Virtues of Man
> without his Vices.
> This Praise, which would be unmeaning flattery
> If inscribed over Human Ashes,
> Is but a just tribute to the Memory of
> 'Boatswain,' a Dog
> Who was born at Newfoundland,
> May, 1803,
> And died at Newstead Abbey
> Nov. 18, 1808.

Although Byron wished to be buried with Boatswain at Newstead, he was eventually laid to rest in the family vault at nearby Hucknall church. Byron had stated that 'Newstead and I stand or fall together', but in view of the deep problems, his advisor John Hanson encouraged him to sell. The situation remained unresolved in 1809 when he departed to travel the Mediterranean. Although Byron returned to England in 1811, he tended to stay with his social set in London. When his mother died he was very distraught as he realised he had neglected her. Over the following years, Byron tried to sell Newstead, but was at first unable to get a fair price. In the spring of 1813, an offer was made and accepted, but the buyer failed to produce the £140,000. Now in desperate financial straits, Byron was still living in expectation of a sale. In part driven by this financial pressure, Byron proposed marriage to the wealthy heiress Anne Isabella Milbanke, but she at first refused him. However, when Byron proposed to Miss Milbanke a second time, in September 1814, she accepted, and on marriage became Lady Byron. In July 1815, Newstead was again for sale, but once more did not meet the reserve price. At this time, the couple lived at Piccadilly Terrace, London, and Byron was increasingly troubled by financial problems. Despite these problems, he still rejected offers for his writing, believing the amounts offered to be too small. Unable to sell the estates at Newstead and Rochdale, he could not clear the debts. By summer 1815, Byron became increasingly angry and violent towards his wife. With his moods dark and depressive, he drank heavily. Later the same year he began an affair with London chorus girl Susan Boyce, and Lady Byron became increasingly distressed by the situation. By now she was late in her pregnancy, and felt Byron was going insane. On 10 December 1815, Lady Byron gave birth to a daughter named Ada, the couple's only child, yet Byron's depressive state worsened. On 21 April 1816, Byron signed the Deed of Separation from Anne, and departed England forever; he never saw Anne or Ada again.

However, a financial solution was at hand; by 1818, a buyer was found. Colonel Thomas Wildman, who had been at Harrow School with Byron and was heir to Jamaican plantations, paid £94,500 for Newstead, and spent a considerable sum on repairs and renovations too. The property was to change hands again, and in 1861, William Frederick Webb, the African explorer, bought the abbey from Wildman's widow. In 1899, after Webb's death, the estate passed to his surviving children, to his grandson Charles Ian Fraser, and then was finally bought and gifted to Nottingham Corporation.

Undoubtedly, the poet Byron was the most significant person connected with Newstead. After the birth of his daughter, Byron and his college friend John Hobhouse, 1st Baron Broughton, left for Italy, arriving on 12 October 1816. He was to stay for six and a half years, and there wrote some of his greatest poetry. They stayed in Milan and met Italy's leading writers, like Monti and Pellico. Indeed, as writers, the two received a level of respect denied them in England. From Milan, they went to Venice, where Byron stayed until 1819. Remarkably, he studied Armenian at San Lazzaro Monastery. Here Byron spent time with two of his most celebrated mistresses, Mariana Segati and Margarita Cogni, both wives of other men, but apparently condoned by Italian society. Following these liaisons, Byron embraced total promiscuity or 'free love'. His friend, the poet Shelley, an advocate of free love, described Byron's behaviour thus:

L[ord] B[yron] is familiar with the lowest sort of these women, the people his gondolieri pick up in the streets. He allows fathers & mothers to bargain with him for their daughters, & though this is common enough in Italy, yet for an Englishman to encourage such sickening vice is a melancholy thing. He associates with wretches who seem almost to have lost the gait & phisiognomy of man, &

do not scruple to avow practices which are not only not named but I believe seldom even conceived in England. He says he disapproves, but he endures.

This behaviour carried on until he became bored of it, triggering the writing of 'We'll go no more a-roving', regarded as a statement of 'post-orgiastic disgust'. Finally, in April 1819, he fell madly in love with someone else's wife, the twenty-one-year-old Teresa Guiccioli. He remained faithful to her until he left for Geneva. Following a further tempestuous period and the death of another daughter, Byron took up the cause of Greek independence from the Ottoman Empire, and set off to Greece with weapons and supplies. However, before he was able to join the uprising, he was struck down by a serious fever. Doctors attending on Byron attempted cures with leeches and castor oil, but in vain, and he fell into a deep stupor. He regained consciousness and stated, 'Now I shall go to sleep. Good night', but then died within the day. The poet Lord Byron died in 1824, a long way from Newstead, and his last words were, 'My daughter! My sister!' On his death, the post-mortem recorded that he had a brain weighing in at 10 pounds, which if true, is around three times the normal size. Byron's heart was cut out and sent to Missolonghi in Greece, where it was buried. Then the rest of his body was despatched to England, where, because of his scandalous lifestyle, he was refused burial in Westminster Abbey. Instead, his remains were laid to rest in the family vault close to Newstead Abbey. In 1969, a memorial to the great poet and philanderer was set into the floor of Westminster Abbey, a reminder of the life, genius, and tragedy of George Gordon, Lord Byron. In many ways, Byron was a unique figure in English history and literature, yet in other ways, he and his Newstead estate seem so typical of the story of the Dukeries and Sherwood.

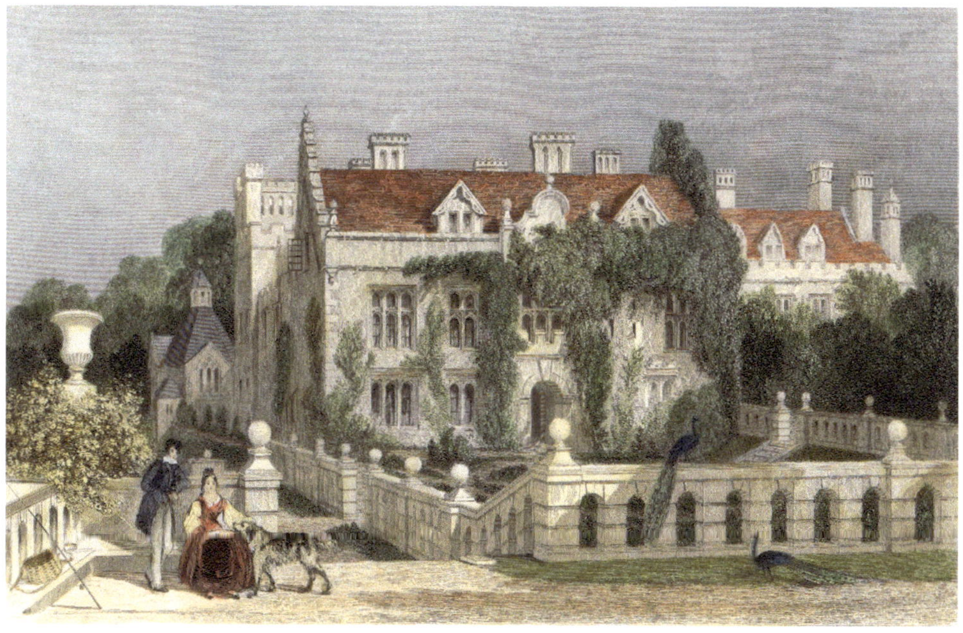

Newstead Abbey, home to 'the' Lord Byron.

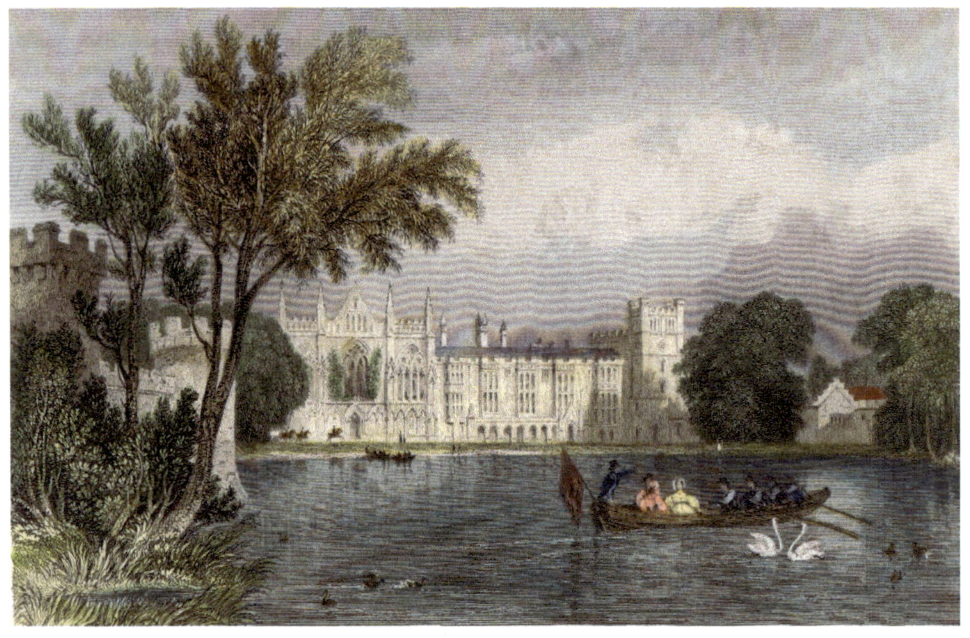

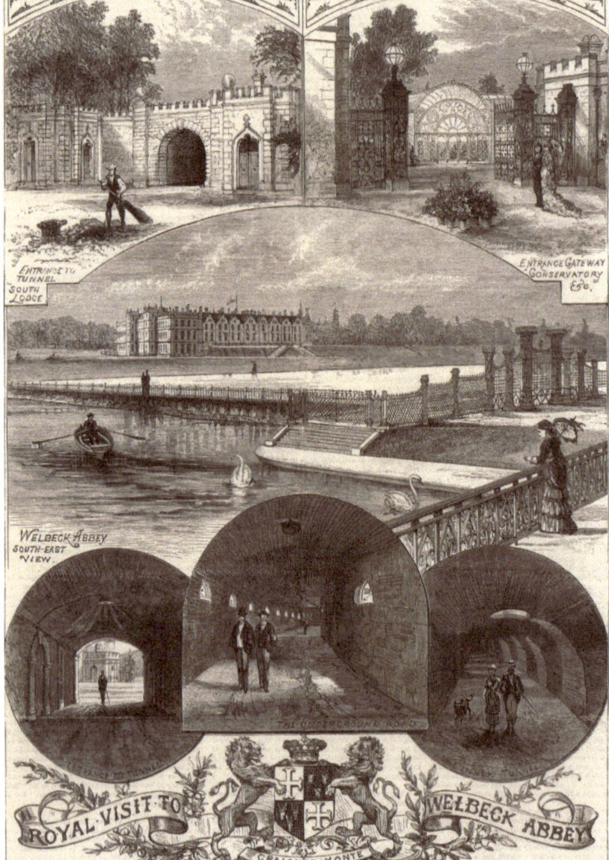

Above: Newstead Abbey with boats and swans.

Left: Welbeck, 1881, from the *Illustrated London News.*

6

A Rural Life: Farming, Hunting and Forestry

This chapter looks at the rural landscapes and their communities mixing the wider farming with the life on the great estates – the farmers and peasants, and the gamekeepers and foresters. There is a way of life that now just about hangs on in a few estates but it was defining and almost unique for many centuries. Today, the daily round of estate life has largely passed, but it lives on in photographs and in the ancient buildings that remain. Interesting relicts of former ways of life show up in ancient field patterns, secret green lanes and hollow ways, ancient hedges, and remarkable features like eighteenth-century water meadows. Much of the region was dominated by open, barren heathland, and where areas were capable of short-term improvement and cultivation, this was followed by abandonment and fallow. The lands capable of cultivation were mostly brecks or brakes, from the Old English word 'braec', 'land which is difficult to cultivate or broken land'. The soils were easy to break and plough but could not sustain long-term agriculture and would revert back to communal grazing and, by medieval times, aristocratic or royal hunting. The big trees, which grew widely spaced in this heathy landscape, were valuable for the construction of buildings and warships.

However, this was not always a landscape or countryside of peace and tranquillity. William Cowper noted that in the eighteenth century, 'improvement was the idol of the age' and 'fed by many a victim'. By the seventeenth century, landowners' thoughts were turning to 'improvement', and both science and technology were beginning to provide the tools to transform the common landscape into both productive farmland and private, grand, landscape parks. In establishing the great estates, the aristocracy often displaced those with common rights. Commoners and peasants became wage-slaves or worse, unemployed and landless. The dispossessed became trespassers and poachers, and the landowners employed armed gamekeepers and mantraps to ruthlessly enforce compliance with their decrees. Even up until recent times, local people might find long-abandoned traps in the woods. These were perfectly legitimate to use, and if the unfortunate victim wishes to complain, the landowner responsible might well be the local magistrate too. The pressure to 'improve' was intensified by events in Revolutionary France and the Napoleonic Wars. A further move, alongside the establishment of grand parks, was to plant 'high forest' woodlands or plantations. By the early 1700s, Daniel Defoe was able to describe the Welbeck Estate as 'nobly wooded'. In Hayman Rooke's 1799 book, he noted the patriotic sentiments behind this move and was able see that efforts were made to 'adorn this ancient Forest in a manner truly patriotic and worthy of imitation'. Much of the landscaping involved the removal of 'wilderness' areas to create plantations and vistas of open land. Beyond the park pale, however, a major move to was to wrest the common heath from both commoner and from its ecology. Although a relatively large amount of the nationally rare lowland heath remains, it is still a pitifully small proportion of what was there originally. However, designers and improvers such as Humphrey Repton approved of what they found on estates like Welbeck; he described it as Portland's 'great stile of improvement'. In part, this was driven by economic and productive necessity, in part by a desire to create or reveal the 'picturesque'. Designers such as Uvedale price stated that there were 'pictures in every tangled wood and thicket when the rubbish is removed'. As a result of all these pressures, the ancient forest and heath were progressively reduced and encroached upon. Some of the most ancient and significant trees were safeguarded, but many more were lost.

Part of the intention of the landowners was to make money and turn what were sometimes costly estates into profitable ventures. A planting scheme required outlay, but could bring a financial return quickly, through, for example, the sale of thinnings for beesom (broom) making. Some of the lower-lying riverside plantations such as at Thoresby were used to produce hop poles for the hop industry located around Retford. Estates also tended to reduce the numbers of deer in their park herds in order to increase numbers of sheep. At Clumber, the park deer were removed and carted to nearby Haughton Park, which became a venison larder, because they interfered with the duke's planting schemes. Clumber became the grassland-dominated estate we see today. In 1793, it had 1,500 acres of grass with 76 acres of clover, 195 acres of turnips, and 100 acres of water meadow. Arable crops also included 210 acres of oats, 76 acres of barley, 67 acres of wheat, and 65 acres of rye. On the arable land, 2,000 sheep of the new Leicestershire breed were 'folded', their dung and urine improving fertility. Similar systems of improvement and husbandry were applied across the Dukeries.

Sherwood Forest was shrinking and by 1790, surveys revealed only 10,117 mature oaks where had been 49,909 in 1609. There was new planting and new roadside avenues of oaks and especially, like in Clumber, of limes. The old landscape was disappearing and a new one, which would pave the way for the modern era, was emerging in its place.

The towns, villages and hamlets reflect the mix of industry with rural. Budby, for example, is a model hamlet built to accommodate the staff and workers of the Thoresby Estate. Close by on a hill is the so-called Budby Castle, actually a modest eighteenth-century part house, part folly once called Castle William. This was built for Evelyn Pierrepont, 2nd Duke of Kingston, to house the crews for a boat called *Mary* that sailed on Thoresby Lake. The house was named after William Scott, 'Captain of the Mary', who died in 1756. The same year, Charles Meadows Pierrepont, 1st Earl Manvers, came to Thoresby. Castle William, designed by John Carr, is recorded in 1816 as still having a crew stationed there, a practice continued up to at least 1851 when 'Captain Percy' resided and was in charge of the boats. It may be that this was more of a maintenance fleet than the extravagant public show of the original boats.

By the late nineteenth century and through the First World War, Castle William became known as Budby Castle; an ivy-covered residence for the various clerks of works for the Thoresby Estate, and today a private dwelling.

The few remaining heaths, though severed from their utilitarian functions as grazing lands and providers of turf fuel and other materials, provide a link back to earlier times. Similarly, the famous open fields of Laxton hint at the medieval system of common agriculture that once dominated this landscape. Parliamentary enclosures of common land, and re-distribution to a few more wealthy local people, transformed the countryside. The heaths and commons are a throwback to the earlier system, as too were the ancient coppice woods that dotted the landscape. Important to local people and the local economy, woods often survived, even under the new system. However, by the nineteenth century and increasingly into the twentieth century, traditional woods and woodmanship gave way to 'forestry', a system of intensive cultivation of often exotic trees such as pines for timber production. This approach, imported to Britain from Continental Europe, received a massive boost after the First World War. With fears for our island cut off from overseas timber supplies, the government of the day established the Forestry Commission. Driven by massive budget subsidies, industrial plantation forestry swept over the landscape. For the sandy soils of the Sherwood heaths, this was a dramatic change, going from open heaths with scattered but massive oak trees, to serried ranks of impenetrable, dense conifers. The legacy remains today and has in part been absorbed into the character of today's Sherwood. Few visitors realise how recent and alien a feature this is.

Current policy is to maintain some areas of productive forest, but at the same time to remove conifers from relict heaths and deciduous woods, and re-establish the fauna and flora so ruthlessly squeezed by forestry plantings. The tall pines and other conifers today provide a backdrop to many recreational and outdoor sporting activities, and a unique habitat for some wildlife species such as fallow deer, which like the plantations.

Free-draining, sandy soils are naturally acidic and low in plant nutrients, but they can be turned to intensive agriculture with modern techniques, chemical fertilisers and, when necessary, irrigation. Although steps have been taken to limit the worst excesses of technologically driven farming, it is unlikely that much converted heathland will ever revert to its former character. The food production from what is now high-grade land will remain important, even though it takes a huge amount of energy and chemicals to maintain the output.

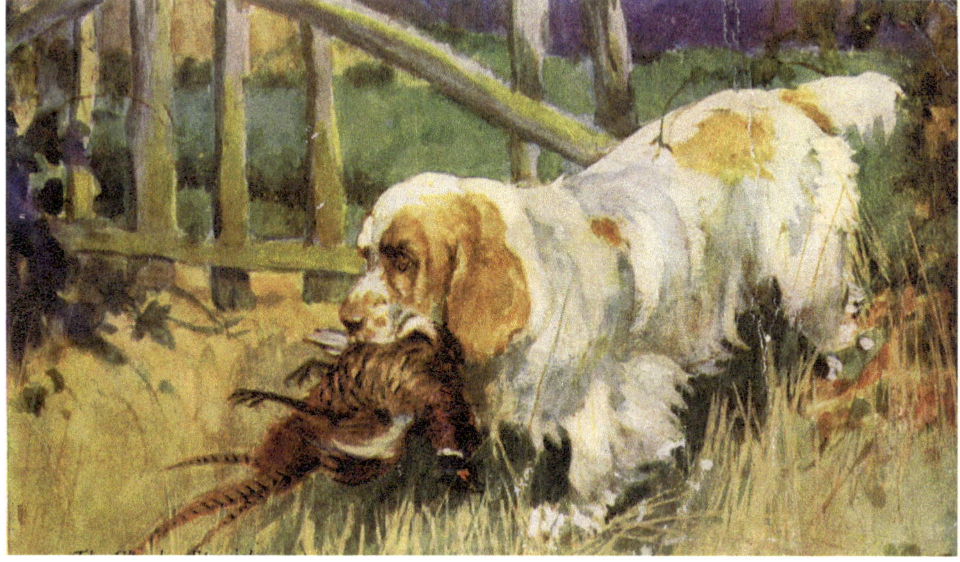

Clumber Spaniel, a local estate breed still popular today.

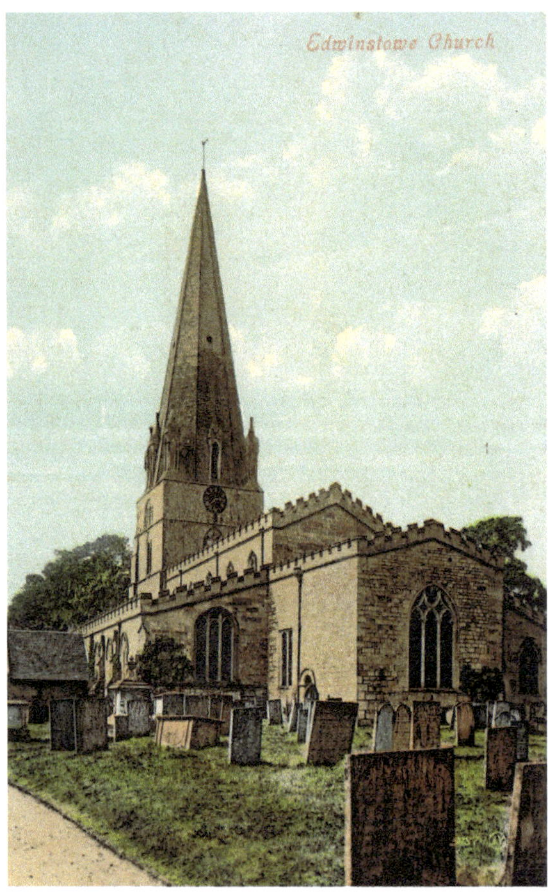

Left: Edwinstowe church, early 1900s.

Below: Lambley church, Nottinghamshire, early 1900s.

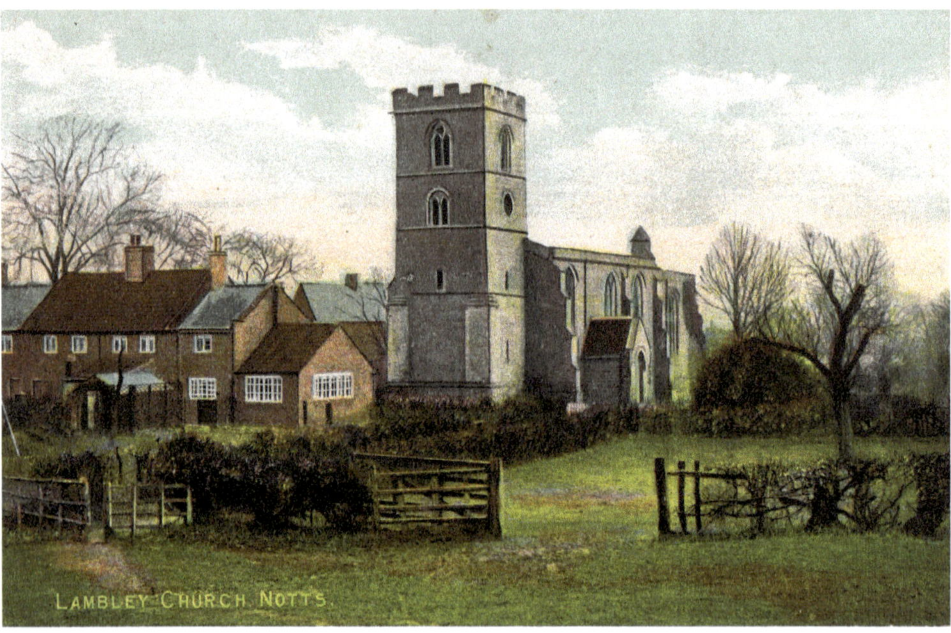

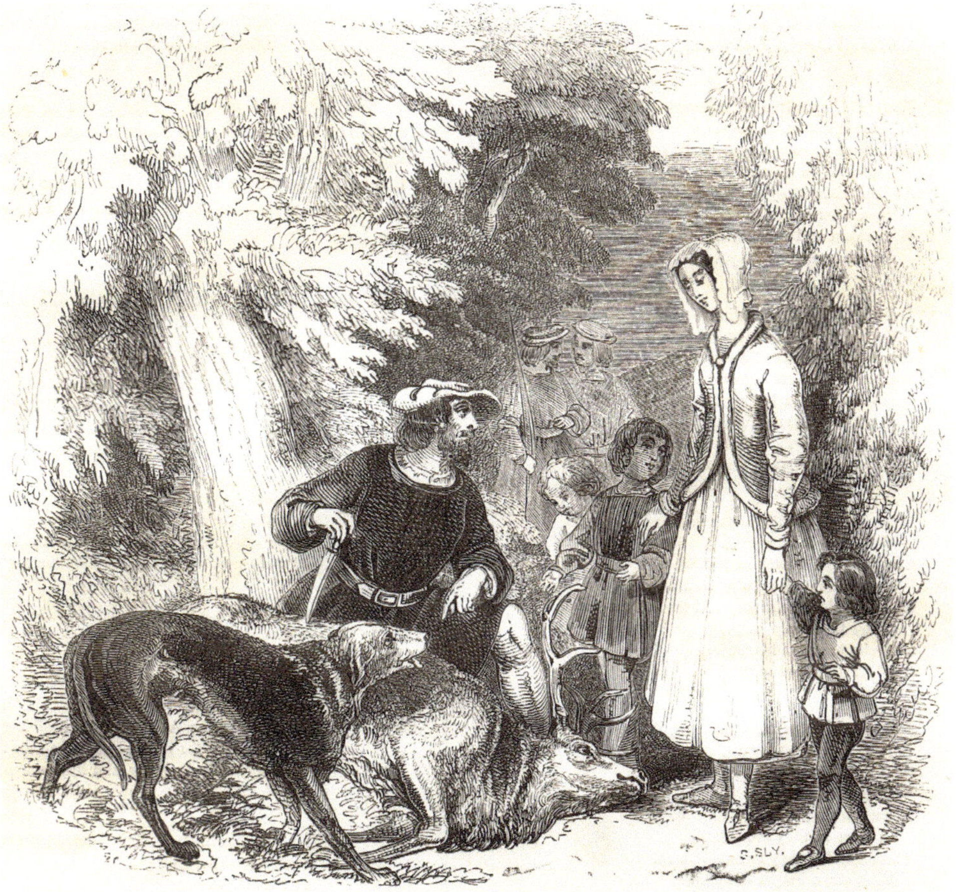

Above: A forest scene from a Victorian print.

Right: Lord George Bentinck in 1848, the year of his sudden and tragic death.

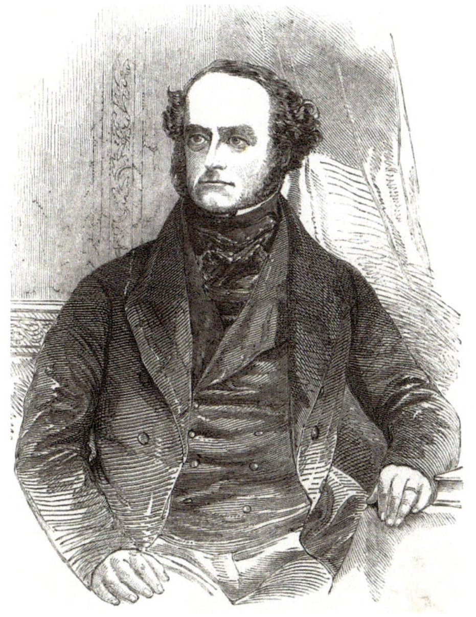

7

INDUSTRY, SETTLEMENT, WAR AND PEACE

Although the rural character of Sherwood and the Dukeries is clear to the visitor, and largely is what they expect, the industrial nature of parts of the region comes as a surprise. Underlying the red sandstones of the Sherwood area are rich mineral resources, particularly coal. This provided incentive and wealth to import skilled workers and establish new mining settlements across the region. The result was the catastrophic transformation of landscapes and communities, with effects still reverberating today. By the 1920s, Britain had over a million men working 'down the pit' and during this time, seven new pits were sunk in the Dukeries. Interestingly, before mining, the area had no significant manufacturing industry. The regional economy centred on the great estates and associated farming, forestry and other activities. Nearly 40 per cent of the region was dominated by individual estates exceeding 10,000 acres. When industrial coal mining came to the region there was a flourishing tourist trade, especially in the summer, focused on the Major Oak, and similar iconic features. The area was described as 'the prettiest stretch of country north of Sussex and south of the Highlands'. However, landowners were quick to spot coal as their economic saviour, to keep them in lavish and luxurious style and fashion in their grand country retreats. For the old, established settlements such as Edwinstowe, Clipstone, Ollerton, and others, the changes were dramatic and even catastrophic. Edwinstowe, for example, had a population of around 1,000 residents, and was a typical rural backwater where things changed slowly, if at all. Coal mining needed skilled labour for the pits and for all the associated industries and activities, and these men and their families were imported. Furthermore, they needed accommodating in new settlements such as the model colliery villages.

New arrivals, both workers and coal mine owners, potentially threatened old ways and old hierarchies, and resentment, still present today, ran deep. The old and the new did not necessarily sit happily side by side. The *Mansfield Reporter* in 1924 ran a feature on Blidworth, which explained how the 'colliery workers have invaded the village and the undefiled air of the parish has been polluted with Bolshevic talk'. The prospect was of 2,000 new houses swamping the old rural community. Schools and other services struggled to keep pace, leading to deep-seated resentment. Eventually, to a large degree, industry and new communities have been assimilated into the unique landscape of the Dukeries, but the scale and speed of the changes were remarkable. By the 1930s, the mines were at full productive capacity and the wealth created was vital for the major landowners. However, by 1938, when the nationalisation of coal royalties was imposed, there was an exodus of the aristocracy from the area. Welbeck became a military training college, Clumber was mostly demolished, Rufford was abandoned, Newstead was sold off and Thoresby became residential flats.

This is too short a book to consider the issues in depth, but these were seismic changes for people and countryside. The construction of mines and villages swept away entire landscapes, and waste slag spewed out over the country. Watercourses and wetland dried up, and those that remained were often grossly polluted. The air was thick and heavy with sulphur and grime. Even hidden below ground, the industry took its toll on the landscape and the buildings, as mining subsidence caused huge problems. Once the coal and 'overburden' was removed, abandoned mine-workings collapsed and the ground sank. You can see the impacts at Clumber Park where the lake extended in recent decades because the land sank. The stark timbers of dead trees, still standing now in the water, mark where land became lake. There were moves to demolish houses such as Thoresby, to allow further expansion of coal extraction. Then, in the 1980s, came the collision between miners and the Thatcher government, and the abrupt end of the once great industry.

The cessation of coal extraction and processing was sudden, abrupt and decisive. With just a few exceptions, almost all the mines closed, with catastrophic effects on people and communities. It seems strange to think that this defining impact on the landscape and on the people of Sherwood and the Dukeries was over and done with in less than a hundred years. In the post-1990s, post-industrial age, despoiled areas are healing and former coaling sites even restored to heathland. Yet the scars and the imprints of century's industry will never fully go.

Alongside the industrial development of the Sherwood region was another major impact and challenge for local, rural communities. Heaths and forests were always good places to train soldiers and Sherwood is no exception to this. The impacts of the Army can be seen across Sherwood Forest and until recently, drivers had to beware of Chieftain tanks trundling across the roads. Sites like the National Trust's Clumber Park were important transit and storage areas for military during the Second World War, and the tank storage bays can still be found in the woods today. The woods and forests also hide sites of Second World War machine-gun posts and other evidence of the networks of defensive lines established should the Nazi Germans invade. Training trenches, foxholes and ammunition dumps are further evidence of wartime occupation.

While military ownership and use of wide-open heaths may seem to be the antithesis of conservation, it is probable that this saved Sherwood and many other sites from an even worse fate in the 1960s and 1970s. Without the military necessity, maintained during the Cold War, it is likely that even more land would have been sucked into intensive farming and even less heath would remain than does so today.

As it was, heathlands such as Sherwood provided ideal locations to practice for battle, used for military training and manoeuvres from as far back as the Crimean War, and maybe even earlier. Open, dry, flat ground was good land to train soldiers and to drill troops. During the Second World War, too, many sites were used for Home Guard activities and training. Hidden in plantations and woods, and on overgrown heaths, the trenches and foxholes of long-forgotten soldiers overlie medieval trackways, park boundaries, and agricultural fields or settlements; each period blending into those that went before.

As with the influx of miners, the military use of the region also involved the mass immigration of outsiders into the area. Just as with miners and their model villages, the military established major camps and training grounds across the region.

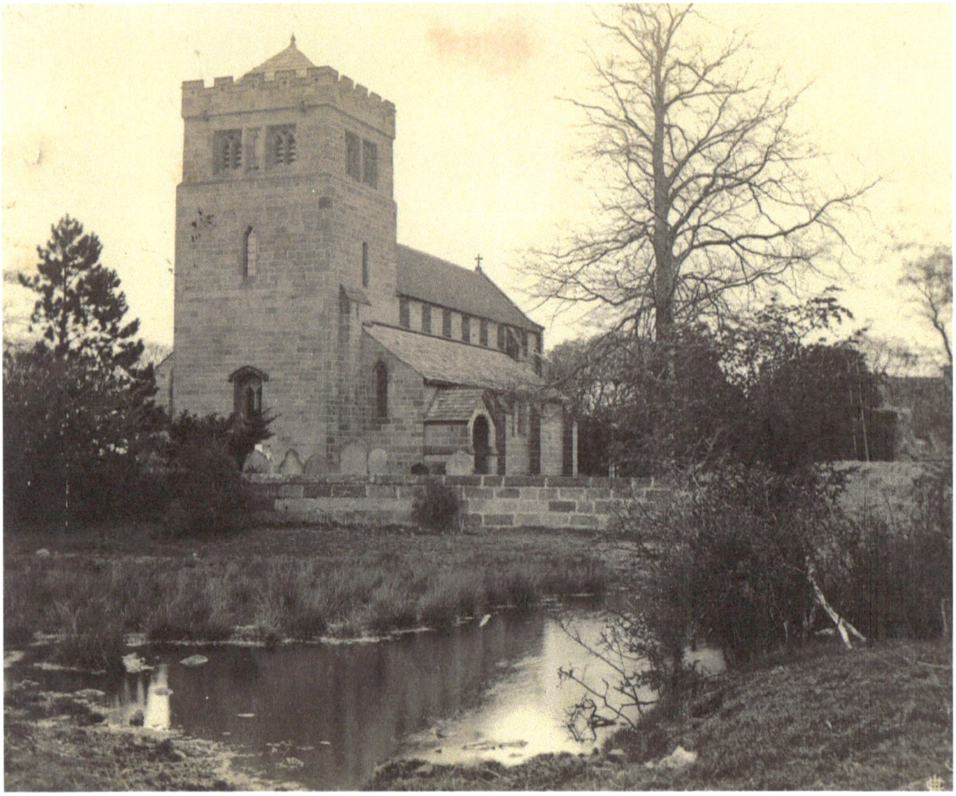

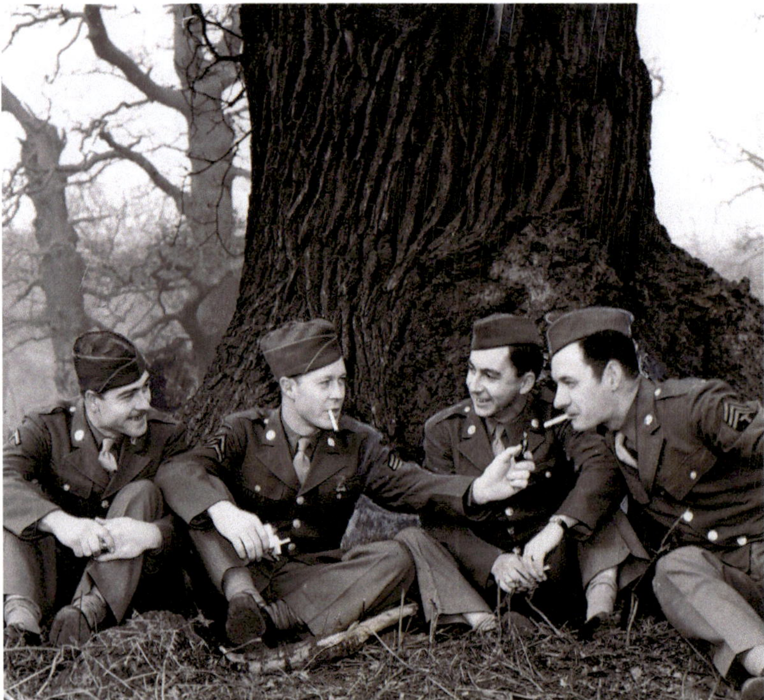

Above: Carlton church, 1904.

Left: Californian soldiers at Sherwood, 1944.

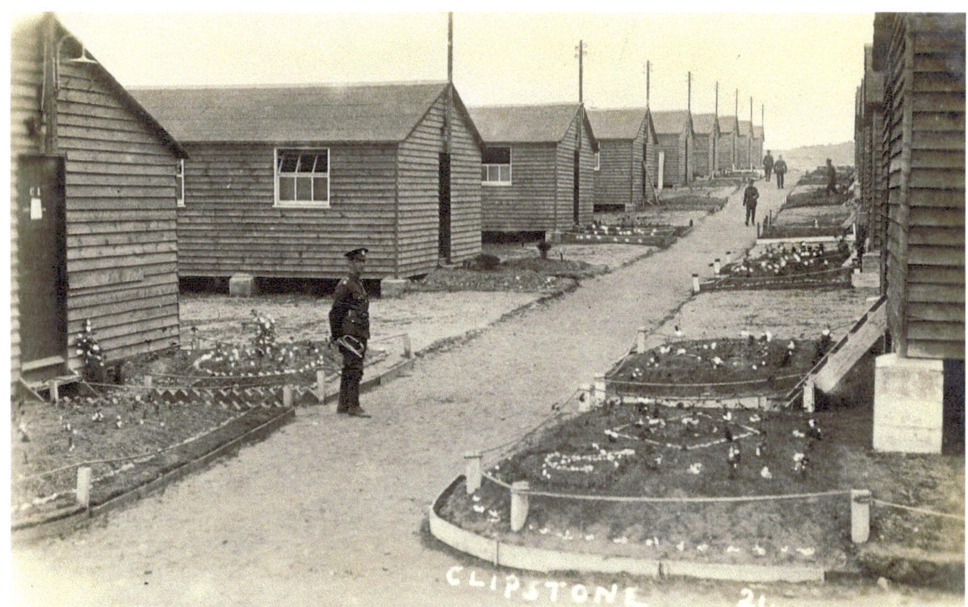

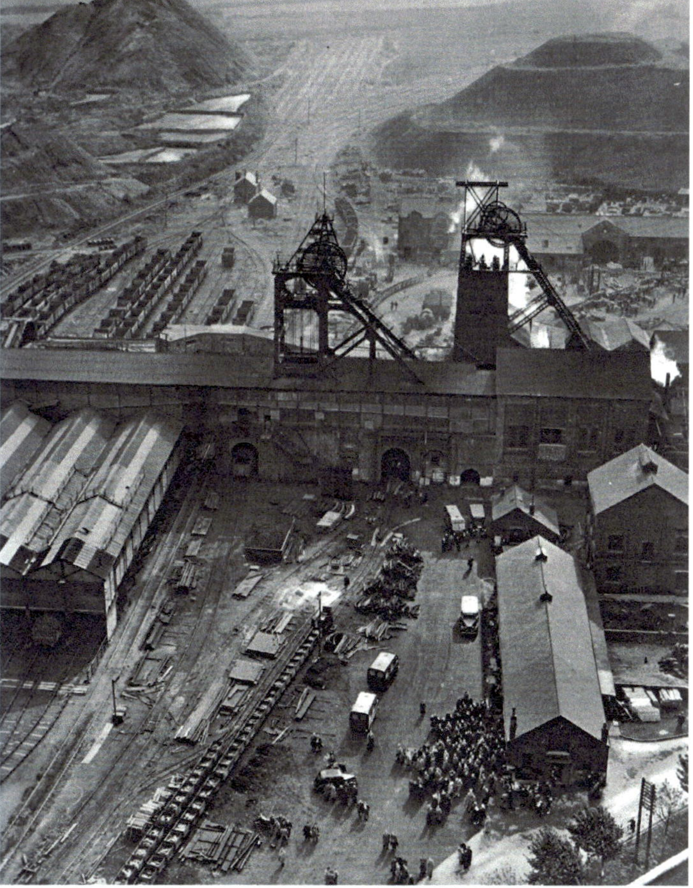

Above: Clipstone Army Camp in 1915 with a scene typical of Sherwood during much of the twentieth century.

Right: Creswell Colliery disaster, October 1950, where eighty miners died in a fire.

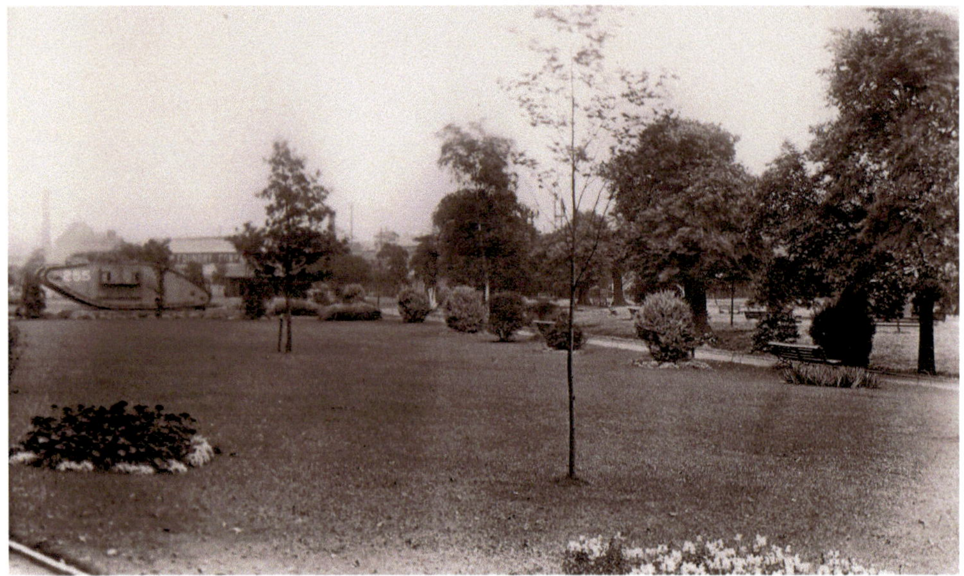

Titchfield Park, Mansfield, 1920s, with First World War tank.

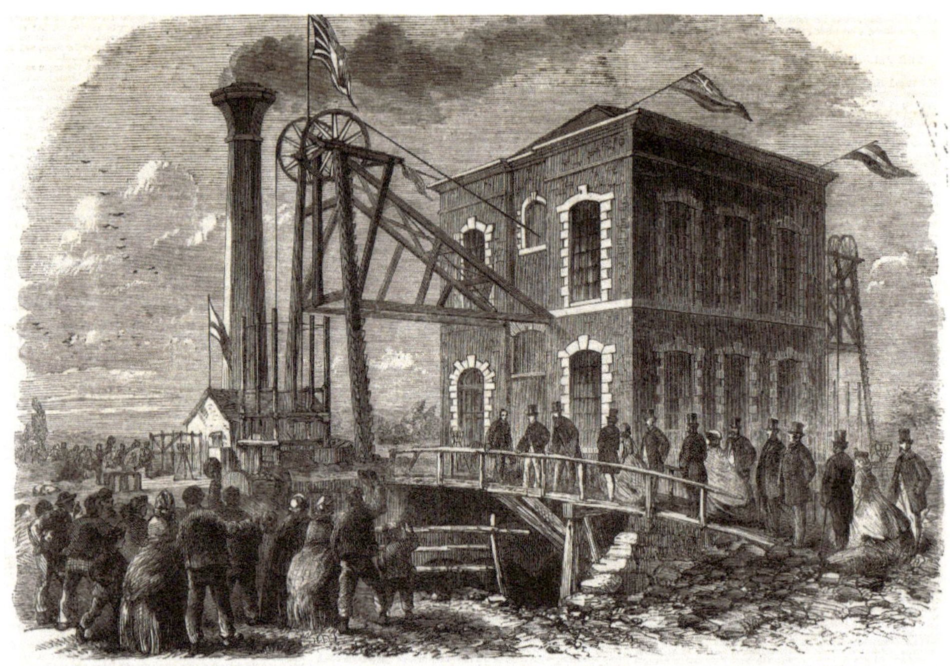

The Prince of Wales at Shireoaks coal mine, property of the Duke of Newcastle, 1861.

8

DECLINE, FALL, RENAISSANCE AND RE-EMERGENCE

From the late nineteenth century, as fashions, politics, and the economy changed, the great houses and estates came under increasing pressure. Furthermore, in some cases the consequences of deep mining were land subsistence and structural problems for buildings or other constructions. One by one, the great houses and their parks were abandoned to a variety of fates. Clumber was demolished to leave the stable-block and the church, and then acquired by the fledgling National Trust in order to prevent further loss. Remarkably, they bought the site through public subscription to save it for the nation and to prevent a local wood-yard from acquiring the rights to the timber. Once the Trust got the site, however, they sold and felled many of the great oaks to help fund the purchase. The cut stumps can still be seen in the ancient woodland of Hardwick Wood. Welbeck remains in private hands, but has spent many decades, up until quite recently, as a military training college. Thoresby, once threatened with demolition by the British Coal Board, was split into flats and is now a luxury spa hotel. Then, in the 1980s and 1990s, the coal mines that had so controversially transformed so much of the landscape and so many of the communities, ended. Like a ghost in the night, the coal mining and the associated industries had gone. Nearly a hundred years of massive impact across the wider region, and a century of gross effects on Sherwood and the Dukeries, stopped abruptly, leaving communities stunned and landscapes despoiled. The glorious and rich countryside of farms, forest, parks, and woods was pockmarked by derelict spoil heaps, abandoned buildings and contaminated lands.

By the Victorian era, Sherwood and the Dukeries were already major tourism locations. Indeed, even during the height of the industrial impacts, the leisure and tourism continued to grow. With the Robin Hood's Sherwood connection, and the great success of locations such as Clumber with the National Trust, the region continues to be a hugely popular destination for both tourism and leisure day visitors.

The region is a great place to view wildlife, from rare birds of woodland or heath, to water birds associated with the rivers and lakes. The abundant walks and trails make visits to the area easy and pleasant too, with the added bonus of a glimpse perhaps of fallow deer or roe deer, and diverse wildflowers or spectacular trees. Furthermore, the visitor can find diverse heritage, from old buildings and halls, to medieval churches, to prehistoric caves. It was this diversity, and a pretty, romantic, picturesque landscape that drew the crowds. It is true that the increased urbanisation and the industrialisation of some parts of the region took its toll.

Nevertheless, this was to some extent compensated for by the increased population living in and around the region, and therefore the rise in potential for local visits. Clumber and Sherwood have been traditional destinations for visitors from the nearby industrial cities of Derby, Nottingham and Sheffield. So even during the darkest days of industrial development, the visitors still came.

However, with the collapse of mining and the closure of associated industries, the region entered a new era. Leisure and tourism, together with farming and forestry, are at the core of this new phase for the region's history. Ideas of a Regional Park for the Sherwood Forest area, and popular attractions such as Center Parcs, locate tourism at the heart of the future developments for the area. Unfortunately, Nottinghamshire County Council lost a considerable amount of money in the collapse of the Bank of Iceland, and the project is on hold. Sometime in the future, however, this vision will become reality, and placed in the very centre of England, close to the M1 motorway and to international airports, Sherwood and the Dukeries are easily accessible to a huge number of people. Now in the post-industrial era, the region is rapidly developing into one of England's premiere tourist destinations. At the very core of this renaissance lies the remarkable natural and historic heritage of the region, and the unique legends that carry the name 'Sherwood' around the world.

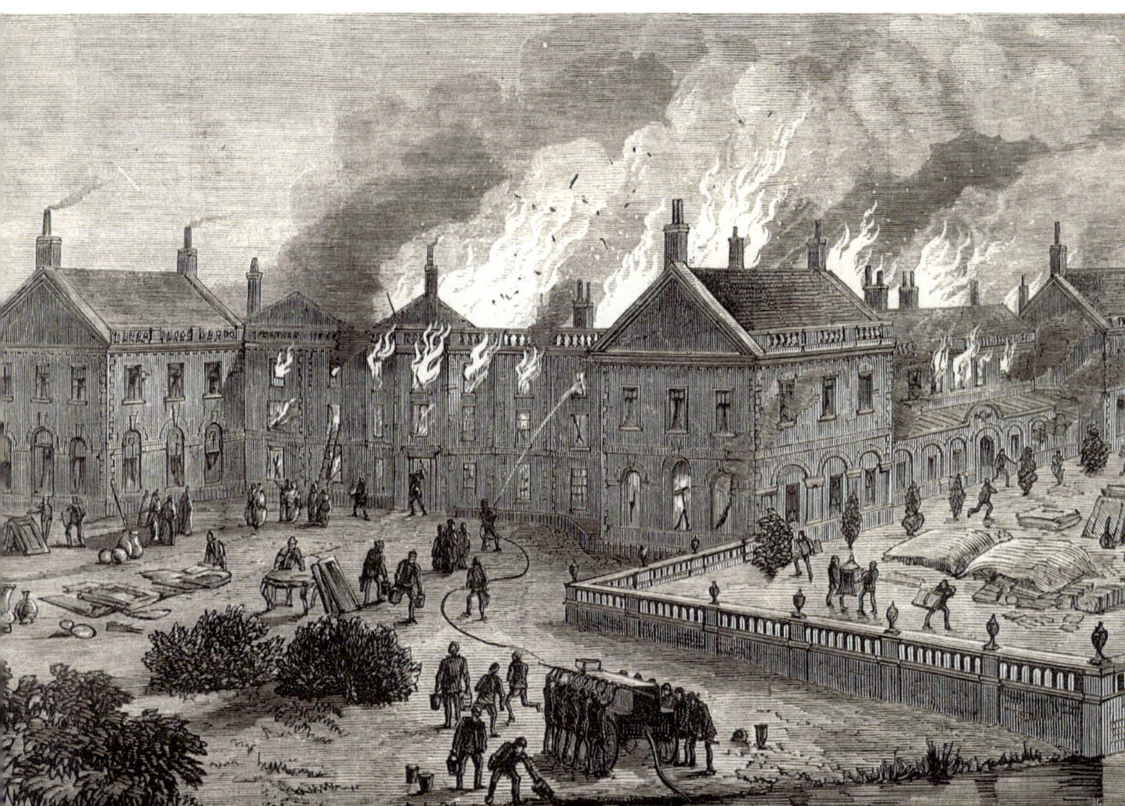

Great houses were often the victims of catastrophic fires as with the fire at Clumber House in 1879.

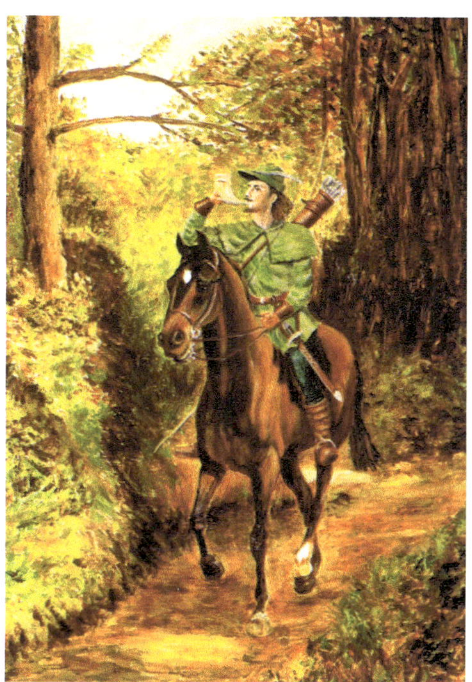

A postcard image from Goaters Limited, Nottingham, of Robin Hood, Prince of Sherwood Forest.

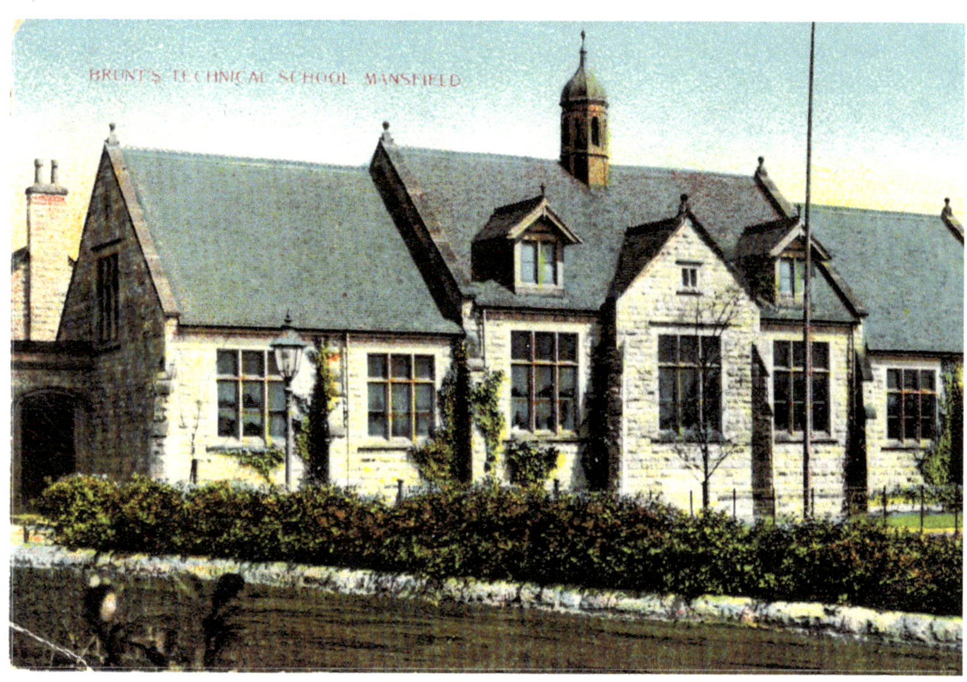

Brunt's Technical School, Mansfield, 1915.

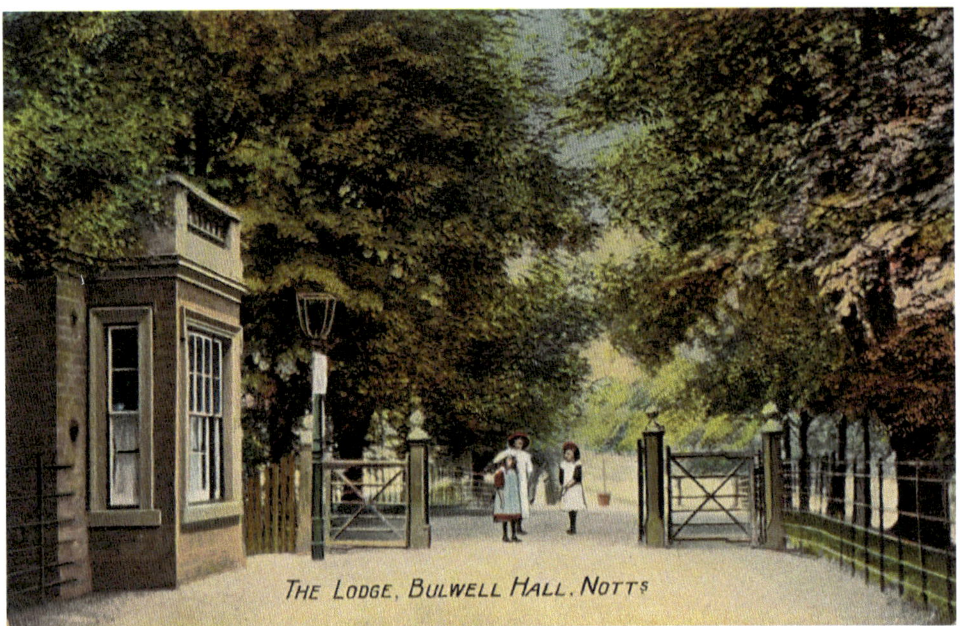

The Dukeries region has numerous smaller halls and houses such as the Lodge, Bulwell Hall, early 1900s.

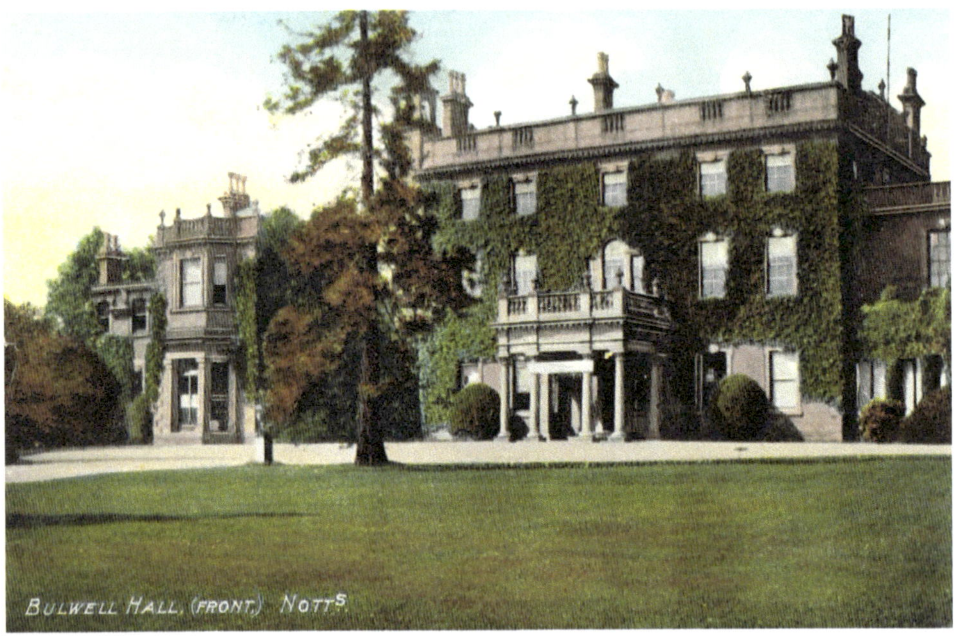

A comfortable country residence, Bulwell Hall, front aspect, early 1900s.

A Remarkable Heritage: Some of the Main Sites and Places

This final chapter provides details of a selection of the main houses, halls, parks, estates, and other tourist locations across the region. The list is not comprehensive and does not make any statement as to the reliability or quality of the individual attractions. Essentially, this gives a flavour of the rich diversity of sites and experiences for the visitor and the local resident.

Amen Corner Karting
Edwinstowe Road
Newark, Rufford
Nottinghamshire, NG22

01623 822205
amencornerkarting.co.uk

Attenborough Nature Centre
Barton Lane, Beeston
Nottingham, NG9 6DY

0115 972 1777
attenboroughnaturecentre.co.uk

Bolsover Castle
Castle Street, Bolsover
Derbyshire, S44 6PR

01246 822844
english-heritage.org.uk

Camping Sherwood Forest
Edwinstowe
Mansfield, NG21 9HW

Center Parcs
Sherwood Forest, Rufford, Newark
Nottinghamshire, NG22 9DN

08448 267 723
www.centerparcs.co.uk

Clumber Park & Gardens (National Trust)
Worksop
Nottinghamshire, S80 3AZ

01909 476 592 / 01909 544917
nationaltrust.org.uk

College Pines Golf Club
Worksop College Drive
Worksop
Nottinghamshire, S80 3AL

01909 501431
collegepinesgolfclub.co.uk

Creswell Crags
Crags Road, Holbeck
Worksop
Nottinghamshire, S80 3LH

01909 720378
creswell-crags.org.uk

Go Ape!
Sherwood Pines Forest Park
Edwinstowe
Nottinghamshire, NG21 9JH

0845 643 9215
goape.co.uk

Hardwick Hall (National Trust)
Doe Lea, Chesterfield
Derbyshire, S44 5QJ

01246 850430
nationaltrust.org.uk

Hodsock Priory
Blyth, Worksop
Nottinghamshire, S81 0TY

01909 591204
hodsockpriory.com

Holocaust Centre
Beth-Shalom
Newark-on-Trent, NG22 0PA

01623 836627
holocaustcentre.net

Isabelle Amante Art Gallery
2 York Terrace
Warsop
Nottinghamshire, NG20 0BL

07970 404599
paintingsbyisabelle.com

Langold Country Park
Langold
Worksop, S81 9QW

01909 730189
bassetlaw.gov.uk

Mansfield Golf Club & Driving Range
Jubilee Way North, Mansfield
Nottinghamshire, NG18 3PJ

01623 422764
mansfieldgolfclub.co.uk

Mr Straw's House (National Trust)
5 Blyth Grove, Worksop
Nottinghamshire, S81 0JG

01909 482380
nationaltrust.org.uk

Newstead Abbey Park & House
Nottingham, NG15 8GE

01623 455 900
newsteadabbey.org.uk

Nottingham Castle
Friar Lane
Nottingham, NG1 6EL

0115 915 3700
nottinghamcity.gov.uk

Ollerton Tourist Information Centre
Worksop Road, Ollerton
Nottinghamshire, NG22 9

01623 824 545
visitnewarkandsherwood.co.uk

Open Water Angling Centre
50 Mansfield Road, Clipstone
Mansfield, NG21 9EQ

01623 627 422
openwaterangling.co.uk

Pond View Moor Farm Caravan Park
Moor Lane, Calverton
Nottingham, NG14 6QT

Rufford Abbey Country Park
Ollerton
Nottinghamshire, NG22 9DF

01623 822944
nottinghamshire.gov.uk

Rufford Abbey English Heritage Site
Ollerton
Nottinghamshire, NG22 9DF

07979 777690
english-heritage.org.uk

Sherwood Castle Holiday Forest
Rufford Lane, Newark
Newark-on-Trent
Nottinghamshire, NG22 9DG

01623 824 400
sherwoodcastle.co.uk

Sherwood Forest Amusement Park

Sherwood Country Park
Edwinstowe, Mansfield
Nottinghamshire, NG21 9QA

01623 823536
sherwoodforestfunpark.com

Sherwood Forest Golf Club

Eakring Road, Mansfield
Nottinghamshire, NG18 3EW

01623 626689
sherwoodforestgolfclub.co.uk

Sherwood Forest Railway

Lamb Pens Lane, Edwinstowe
Nottinghamshire, NG21 9HL

01623 515339
sherwoodforestrailway.com

Sherwood Forest Visitor Centre

Swinecote Road, Edwinstowe
Nottinghamshire, NG21 9HN

01623 823202
nottinghamshire.gov.uk

The Harley Gallery

Welbeck, Worksop
Nottinghamshire, S80 3LW

01909 501700
harleygallery.co.uk

Sherwood Pines Forest Park

Edwinstowe
Nottinghamshire, NG21 9JL

01623 822447
forestry.gov.uk

Southwell Minster

Church Street, Southwell
Nottinghamshire, NG25 0HD

01636 812649
southwellminster.org

Streamline Fishing

Forest Road
New Ollerton, Newark
Nottinghamshire, NG22 9QT

01623 869363

The Workhouse (National Trust)

Upton Road, Southwell
Nottinghamshire, NG25 0PT

01636 817 260
nationaltrust.org.uk

Thoresby Park Courtyard & Riding Hall

Park and Mill
Thoresby Park, Newark
Nottinghamshire NG22 9EP

01623 822365
thoresby.com

Wheelgate Theme Park

White Post Island
White Post
Newark, NG22 8HX

01623 882773
wheelgatepark.com

Wollaton Hall Museum & Park

Wollaton Park
Wollaton
Nottingham, NG8 2AE

0115 915 3900
nottinghamcity.gov.uk

Worksop Golf Club

Windmill Lane, Worksop
Nottinghamshire, S80 2SQ

01909 477731
worksopgolfclub.com

Worksop Tourist Information Centre

Memorial Avenue, Worksop
Nottinghamshire, S80 2BP

01909 501148
bassetlaw.gov.uk

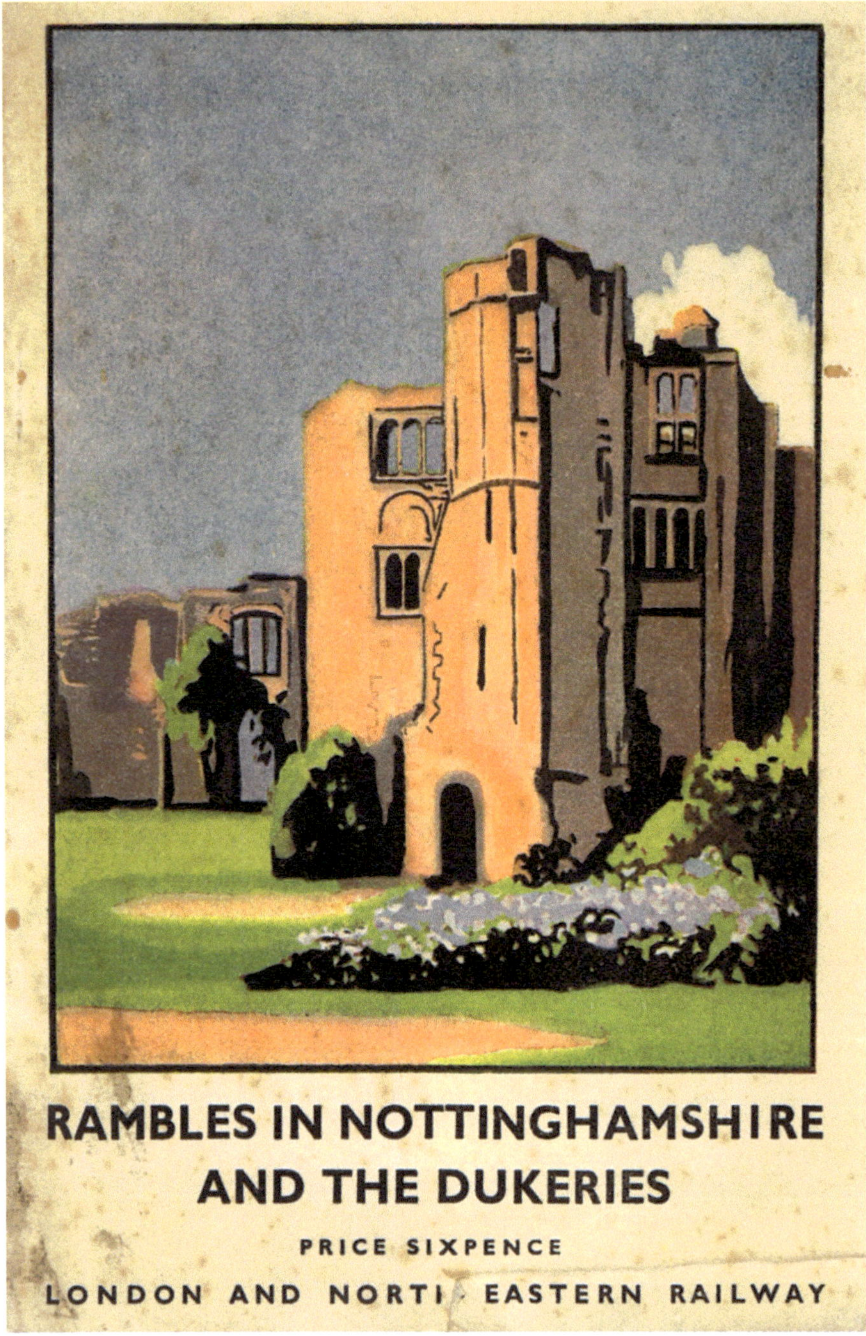

Rambles in Nottinghamshire and Sherwood.

Bibliography

The following are suggested sources and further reading. For the seriously inclined, the publications of the county's Thoroton Society are well worth seeking out.

Anon., *Worksop – The Gateway to the Dukeries* (Worksop: Sissons & Son, undated).
Bealby, J. et al., *A Celebration of Kings Clipstone – 1000 Years of History* (2nd edn, Tuxford, Notts: Acorn Maltone Ltd, 2005).
Eddison, E., *History of Worksop with Historical Descriptive and Discursive Sketches of Sherwood Forest and the Neighbourhood* (1854).
Fletcher, J., *Where Truth Abides. The Diaries of the 4th Duke of Newcastle-Under-Lyme (1822–1850)* (Little Longstone, Derbyshire: Country Books, 2005).
Fletcher, J., *Ornament of Sherwood Forest. From Ducal Estate to Public Park* (Little Longstone, Derbyshire: Country Books, 2001).
Gray, A., *Sherwood Forest and the Dukeries* (Chichester: Phillimore & Co. Ltd., 2008).
Haslehurst, E. W., W. Jerrold and R. M. Gilchrist, *Our Beautiful Homeland* (London: The Gresham Publishing Company, *c.* 1915).
Heywood, J., *John Heywood's Illustrated Guide to the Dukery & Worksop* (Manchester: John Heywood, 1894).
Innes-Smith, R., *The Dukeries and Sherwood Forest* (Derby: English Life Publications, 1984).
Innes-Smith, R., *The Essential Guide to the Dukeries & Sherwood Forest* (Derby: Heritage House Group Ltd., 2002).
Kaye, D., *A History of Nottinghamshire* (Chichester: Phillimore & Co. Ltd., 1987).
Mellors, R., *In and About Nottinghamshire. A Book for the Young Men and Women of the City and County* (Nottingham: J. & H. Bell, 1908).
Redfern, R. A., *The Dukeries of Nottinghamshire* (Skipton: Dalesman Books, 1974).
Reeves, B., *Rambles in Nottinghamshire and the Dukeries* (London: London & North Eastern Railway, undated).
Seymour, S., 'The Dukeries Estate: Improving Land and Landscape in the Later Eighteenth Century', *Transactions of the Thoroton Society of Nottinghamshire*, 97 (1993), 117–128.
Sissons, F., *Sissons' Beauties of Sherwood Forest. Guide to the Dukeries and Worksop* (Worksop: Sissons & Son, 1896).
Sissons, F., *Views of the Dukeries, Sherwood Forest and Worksop* (Worksop: Sissons & Son, *c.* 1880).
Taylor, K., *Exploring Nottinghamshire* (Stroud: Amberley Publishing, 2010).
Waller, R. J., 'Between Two Worlds; Contemporary Reactions to the Arrival of Mining in the Dukeries, 1913–1939' *Transactions of the Thoroton Society of Nottinghamshire*, 84 (1980), 73–80.
Waller, R. J., *The Dukeries Transformed: The Social and Political Development of a Twentieth-Century Coalfield*, Oxford Historical Monographs (Oxford: Clarendon Press, 1983).
Weir, C., *The Nottinghamshire Heritage* (Chichester: Phillimore & Co. Ltd., 1991).
White, R., *Worksop, The Dukery and Sherwood Forest* (London: Ackermann & Co., 1875).

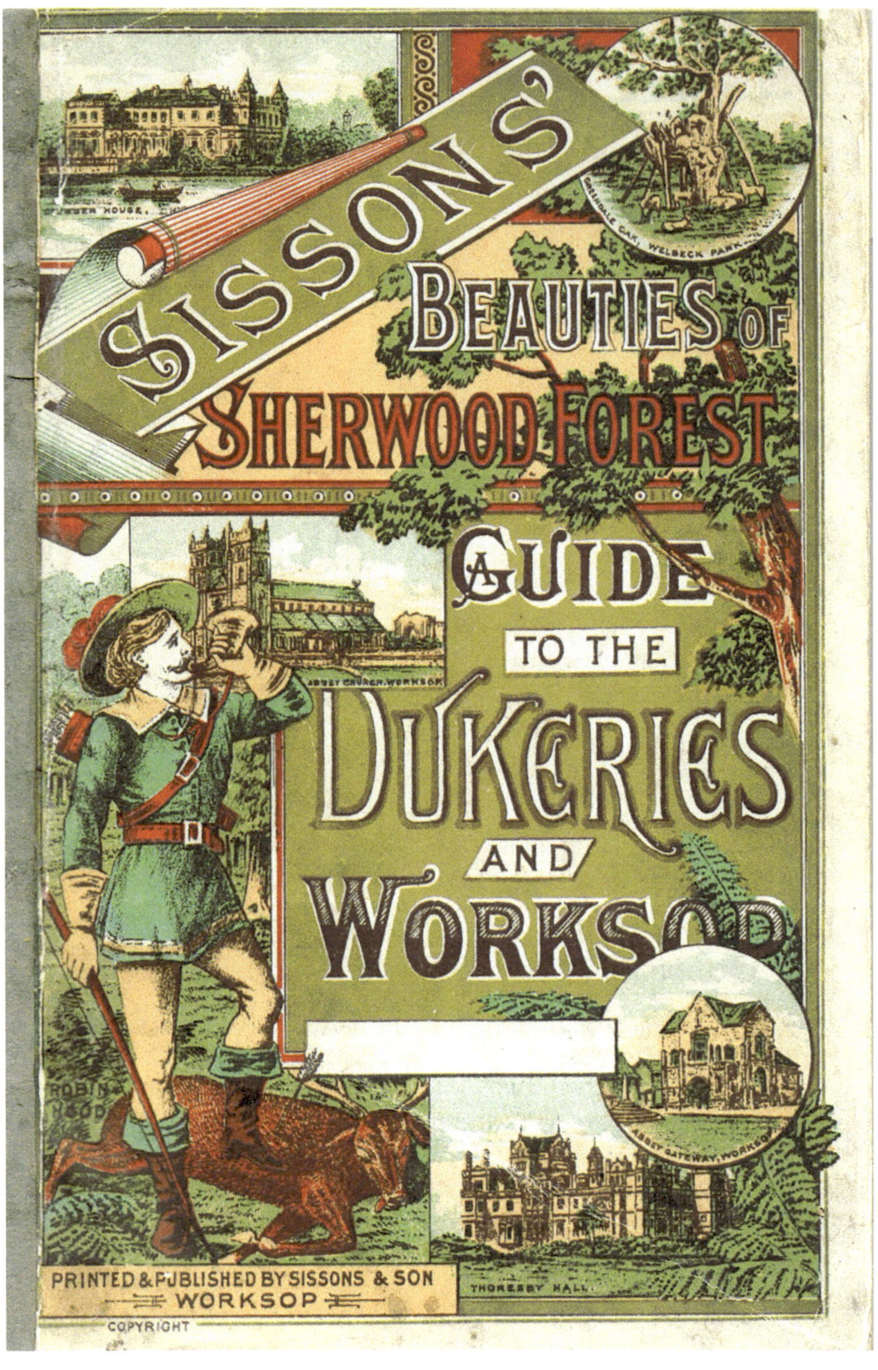

Sisson's *Beauties of Sherwood Forest*.

The majority of images in this book have been taken from the author's own collection. The author has made every effort to seek permission from copyright holders where appropriate. If you have any queries about images appearing in this book, please contact the publishers.